In Memoriam   Sybil H. Milton

October 6, 1941 – October 1

...because we are human, we are prisoners of the years.

Yet that very prison is the room of discipline in which we,

driven by the urgency of time, create.

Gates of Prayer: The New Union Prayerbook

(New York, 1975)

Unknown Photographer

A bystander (far left) watches Jewish deportees on the road in winter, either from Bauschowitz (Bohusovice) to Theresienstadt, or en route from Theresienstadt to killing centers in the East. Systematic deportations to Theresienstadt of entire families, including young children, had begun in early 1942. In June, 1943, a rail spur from Bauschowitz to Theresienstadt was completed.

nd., *The Jewish Museum, Prague, #24.755, 24.764/2, 24.758/1   n.b. Three photographs have been merged.*

ART, MUSIC AND EDUCATION AS STRATEGIES FOR SURVIVAL:

THERESIENSTADT

1941-45

Selected papers from the symposium

ART, MUSIC AND EDUCATION

AS STRATEGIES FOR SURVIVAL: THERESIENSTADT 1941–45

held at Moravian College   Bethlehem, Pennsylvania

February 10–11, 2000

and a catalog of the exhibition

THE ARTS AS STRATEGIES FOR SURVIVAL:

THERESIENSTADT 1941–45

held at Payne Gallery of Moravian College

February 10–March 5, 2000

Essays by Sybil H. Milton, Anne D. Dutlinger, Michaela Hájková,
Hannelore Wonschick, Susan Leshnoff, Rebecca Rovit, and Vojtěch Blodig

Curated and edited by Anne D. Dutlinger

Herodias

New York   London

Portal to exhibition, designed by Timothy Averill,
inspired by a painting by Bedřich Fritta, Theresienstadt, 1943

ART, MUSIC AND EDUCATION AS
STRATEGIES FOR SURVIVAL:

1941–45

THERESIENSTADT

This book is published in cooperation with the Payne Gallery of Moravian College, 1200 Main Street, Bethlehem, PA 18018-6650

Published by Herodias, Inc., 346 First Avenue, New York, NY 10009
Herodias, Ltd., 24 Lacy Road, London, SW15 1NL
www.herodias.com

Manufactured in Hong Kong

Design by Anne D. Dutlinger
Design and production assistance by Stephanie Frey and Rachana Sheth

LIBRARY OF CONGRESS CATALOGING-IN-PUBLICATION DATA

Art, music and education as strategies for survival: Theresienstadt 1941–45/ Anne D. Dutlinger, editor; with essays by Sybil H. Milton, Michaela Hájková.— 1st ed.

     p.cm.

Catalog of an exhibition that opened at the Payne Gallery of Moravian College in February 2000.

Includes bibliographical refrerences and index.

ISBN 1–928746–10–1

1. Children's art—Czechoslovakia—Terezín (Severoéeska kraj)—Exhibitions.
2. Jewish children in the Holocaust—Czechoslovakia—Terezín (Severoéeska kraj)—Exhibitions.
3. Friedl Dicker-Brandeis, 1899–1944—Exhibitions. 4. Theresienstadt (Concentration camp)—Exhibitions. 5. Art therapy for children.
I. Dutlinger, Anne D., 1950– II. Moravian College. Payne Gallery.

N352.2.C95 A78 2000
704'.9240437—dc21   00-026786

BRITISH LIBRARY CATALOGUING IN PUBLICATION DATA

A catalogue record of this book is available from the British Library

Cloth Edition: ISBN 1–928746–10–1
Trade Paperback Edition: ISBN 1–928746–11–X
135798642

First edition 2001

Ela Stein Weissberger (Room 28)
Watercolor on paper
Born June 30, 1930
Deported to Terezín
February 12, 1942
Survived
The Jewish Museum, Prague
#129.186

CONTENTS

AFTERWORD

Ivo Katz
Watercolor on paper
Born April 11, 1932
Deported to Terezín
July 13, 1943
Deported to Auschwitz
December 18, 1944
Perished

The Jewish Museum, Prague
#133.357

ACKNOWLEDGMENTS

Anne D. Dutlinger and Timothy Averill
Slate, steel, chalk, art supplies
February 2000
3.5' x 30"
Photograph by Stephen M. Barth

This exhibition and book could not have been written without the help of many institutions and individuals. I would like to thank The Helen Bader Foundation, Inc. Their generous grant supported the research and development of the exhibition and symposium. Additional funding was provided by Moravian College. Exhibition space, personnel, and partial funding was generously provided by the Payne Gallery of Moravian College, directed by Dr. Diane Radycki. I am grateful to Michelle and David Bader for their interest in the project, to the Development Office at Moravian College and Jill Muchin Zimmerman at The Helen Bader Foundation for their guidance. Thanks go to Rabbi Norman Patz and the Temple Sholom of West Essex, New Jersey, and the Jewish Federation of the Lehigh Valley in Allentown for additional gifts.

Lenders to the exhibition included, in the Czech Republic, the Jewish Museum in Prague, the Terezín Memorial Museum, and the Theater Department of the National Museum in Prague; in the United States, the Leo Baeck Institute in New York and the Simon Wiesenthal Museum of Tolerance in Los Angeles; in Israel, Beit Terezín in Givat Haim. I would like to thank the following private collectors: Ela Weissberger, Georg Schrom, Joža Karas, and Anna Flach Hanusová.

Special acknowledgments go to the numerous institutions and individuals who provided photographs and facilitated permissions to exhibit and publish them: Štěpán Kovařík, archivist at the Jewish Museum in Prague, Terezín Memorial; Anne Millin and Genya Markon of the U.S. Holocaust Memorial Museum; Heidrun Klein, deputy director of Bildarchiv Preussuscher Kulturbesitz in Berlin; Anouk Bellaoud of the Comite de la Croix Rouge; the Bauhaus Archiv in Berlin; Dr. Ernest Zeigler of the City Archives in St. Gallen, Switzerland; Yad Vashem; the Czechoslovak News Agency in Prague; Wallstein Verlag in Göttingen, Germany; Doris Rauch for the estate of Norbert Troller; Prof. Jeremy Adler in London; Solomon R. Guggenheim Museum; Estate of Johannes Itten; Dr. Marik Bolzik of YIVO Institute for Jewish Research in New York; James Hauser; Stephen M. Barth; Ela Weissberger; Anna Flach Hanusová; Helga Weissová-Hosková; Handa and Orni Drori; Vera Nath; Estate of Georg Schrom; Thomas Fritta-Haas; Hilde Angelini-Kothny; Judith Adler; Hannelore Wonschick; Joža Karas; private collectors.

The dedicated assistance of Michaela Hájková, curator of the painting and graphics collection at the Jewish Museum in Prague, was a crucial component of the exhibition at Moravian College. Dr. Vojtěch Blodig, deputy director of the Terezín Memorial, provided

The Arts as Strategies for Survival: Theresienstadt 1941–45 at Payne Gallery of Moravian College, Bethlehem, PA
Photograph by Stephen M. Barth

information and images. Dr. Vlasta Koubska, curator of the theater collection at the National Museum in Prague, provided František Zelenka's scenographic and costume designs.

I am indebted to Sybil H. Milton, whose expertise, scholarship, and editing made significant contributions to our exhibition and this book. Her critical intelligence shaped my research, writing, and design. As we began our first revisions to this book, Sybil fell ill. Her guidance was keenly missed during its corrections and redesign. Her influence, encouragement, and integrity, cut short by an untimely death, is deeply felt by many.

The exhibition could not have occurred without the assistance and advice of Peter Rafaeli, Honorary Consul-General of the Czech Republic in Philadelphia. His countless interventions and support enabled artwork crucial to our exhibition to clear customs in time for the opening—no small task. I will always be grateful to Petr Gandalovič,

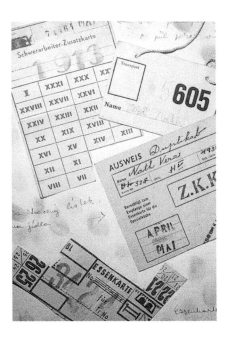

Page from Vera Nath's
(Room 28) Terezín
scrapbook
Courtesy of Vera Nath Kriener

Consul-General of the Czech Republic in New York, for his enthusiasm, ideas, and patience.

For red-tape cutting and moral support I thank Dr. Ervin Rokke, President of Moravian College, Michael Seidl and Dennis Domchek, Vice-Presidents of Moravian College, and Dr. Rudy Ackerman, Chairman of the Art Department of Art at Moravian College.

Ideas and materials were provided by Vojtěch Blodig, Jonathan Fineberg, Michaela Hájková, Joyce Hinnefeld, Larry Lipkis, Rebecca Rovit, Vlasta Koubska, Larry Silberstein, Renata Stein, Mark Talisman, Hannelore Wonschick, Ela Weissberger and "the Girls from Room 28," and Hans-Martin Wuerth.

Many thanks to Paul C. Williams, and Herodias, Inc. for publishing and promoting this book.

The development of the exhibition and this book are especially indebted to Elena Makarova's work on Friedl Dicker-Brandeis. A large-scale retrospective exhibition, *The Art and Soul of Friedl Dicker-Brandeis, Light Defining Darkness,* organized by Regina Seidman of the Simon Wiesenthal Museum of Tolerance and curated by Elena Makarova, will open in the United States in October 2001. A special note of thanks goes to Regina Seidman for introducing me to Michaela Hájková, Curator of the Jewish Museum in Prague, and Ela Weissberger and the rest of "Friedl's Girls" from Room 28.

For their help with producing the exhibition and symposium, thanks go to the Art Department at Moravian College, Jan Ciganick, Nancy Clark, Blair Flintom, Sandy Fluck, Joanne Grandi, Carolyn Katwan, Corinne Lalin, Genevieve LaVo, David Leidich, the Media Center at Moravian College, Matthew Lesniak, Larry Lipkis, Cammie Mojadidi, Fama Mor, Lara Muth, Rose Panik, Shirley Ratushney, Larry Silberstein, Jill Schwab, Deb Smull, Ryan Purdy, Anita Tarsi, and Susan Wooley.

To my students, colleagues, friends, and family, thank you for your patience. Special thanks must be given to Stephanie Frey and Rachana Sheth, two of my graphic design students.

Without their design and production assistance on both the exhibition and catalog, neither the opening nor the press date could have been met.

My husband, Timothy Averill, was both a partner in the design and production of the exhibition and my chief caretaker. I am grateful for his talent and tolerance.

Thanks to Hans-Martin Wuerth, whose study trip on the Holocaust led me back to the children of Terezín.

For the presence of the original children's art from Theresienstadt in the exhibition, much credit is due to my mother, whose influence made me almost incapable of heeding the warning, "It is impossible."

My last thank you, one which cannot be received, goes to my father, whose troubled memories of time spent as a young surgeon at the liberation of Dauchau and Nordhausen fueled my need to tell this story. His gift to me, when I was twelve, *The Diary of Anne Frank*, altered my view of the world.

Anne D. Dutlinger, Curator

Ivan Vojtěch Fric
Transport of Dutch Jews enters the central courtyard, or *schleuse*, February 1944
United States Holocaust Memorial Museum
w/s #20256

Josef Pollak
Pencil on paper
Born January 27, 1933
Deported to Terezín
December 9, 1942
Deported to Auschwitz
May 18, 1944
Perished

The Jewish Museum, Prague
#121.960

PREFACE

In the spring of 2000 the Frank E. and Seba B. Payne Gallery of Moravian College was proud to present *The Arts as a Strategy for Survival: Theresienstadt 1941–45*, a rare exhibition of works by the children of the Theresienstadt ghetto and their teacher, Friedl Dicker-Brandeis (1898–1944).

During the last four years of her life, Dicker-Brandeis passed on to her many students the influences of her own Bauhaus teachers and mentors— Johannes Itten, Walter Gropius, Paul Klee, and Vasily Kandinsky. Also included in the exhibition were works by other artists imprisoned in Theresienstadt— František Zelenka, Norbert Troller, Otto Ungar, and Josef Spier—and archival documents, photographs, and memorabilia lent by several survivors of Theresienstadt.

This exhibition was grounded in the theme of the transforming power of art and art education, and it was an appropriate exhibition for an educational institution such as Moravian College. Moravian has long had a commitment to the arts. The Priscilla Payne Hurd Center is dedicated entirely to music and art. In addition, its Art Department offers a track in Art Education, as well as in Studio Art, Graphic Design, and Art History. Last, but not least, is its art gallery.

Payne Gallery is the jewel in the Priscilla Payne Hurd Center for Music and Art. Made possible by the extraordinary generosity of Priscilla Payne Hurd, the gallery is an unusual asset for a small college. Mrs. Hurd's interest in our students is reflected in the exhibition program of the gallery, which is conceived as an integral part of the college and its academic mission. Designed with our art students in mind, the full program rotates on a four-year cycle in concert with their course of study. Payne Gallery's program supports the offerings of the Art Department, as well as other departments in the college, and reaches out to other art and educational institutions.

Moravian College and Payne Gallery extend our welcome to the many worlds of scholarship and personal memory joined here in *Art, Music and Education as Strategies for Survival: Theresienstadt 1941–45*.

Dr. Diane Radycki
Director, Payne Gallery of Moravian College

Time is inexorable. Only a very few of today's generation can imagine at all the conditions to which prisoners of the concentration camps were exposed. Many of us do not even know to what absolute perfection the totalitarian Nazi regime developed the art of cruelty and the humiliation of mankind.

Thousands of prisoners who experienced the concentration camp Theresienstadt during the Second World War soon realized that they were intended for liquidation. In spite of this, and even in the factories of death themselves, there existed a spark of hope. From that spark was ignited the fire of faith in victory, transformed into the shape of art. These are not the products of salon artists; rather, they are a testimony to a period in time, the reflex of an attempt to bear witness to a horrifying reality, and above all, an expression of the most basic longing—for life, and for a better world. The exhibition that Moravian College prepared along with the Terezín Memorial and the Jewish Museum in Prague sends a symbolic message to all future generations that man must not succumb, even in the most difficult of circumstances. As Ernest Hemingway wrote, "Man can be destroyed, but not defeated."

May this exhibit serve as a reminder of all those who did not give up—the survivors. May it also serve as an appeal to humanity never to tolerate totalitarianism over democracy, and as a memorial to all who consecrated their most precious possession—their own lives—to the fight of good over evil.

H.E. Alexandr Vondra

Ambassador of the Czech Republic
to the United States

Eva Wollsteiner
Collage
Born January 24, 1931
Deported to Terezín
August 4, 1942
Deported to Auschwitz
October 23, 1944
Perished

The Jewish Museum, Prague
#133.357

Eva Riess
Collage
Born July 25, 1931
Deported to Terezín
May 15, 1942
Survived

The Jewish Museum, Prague
#133.357

ART, MUSIC AND EDUCATION AS
STRATEGIES FOR
SURVIVAL:

THERESIENSTADT: 1941-45

Alice Guttman
Pencil on paper
Born September 19, 1928
Deported to Terezín
September 6, 1943
Perished

The Jewish Museum, Prague
#131.753

ART AND ARTISTS IN THERESIENSTADT: QUESTIONS OF SURVIVAL

In spite of the inhumane conditions in Theresienstadt, the cultural life was rich. Literary evenings, concerts, theater performances, and lectures were held in the dormitories, in the lofts, and in the courtyards. There were many artists and scientists in Theresienstadt; the culture was of high standard and the people, including children, took a great interest in it. It was a source of hope and gave people strength to live on.[1]

Hanuš Klauber
Collage
Born January 24, 1929
Deported to Terezín
February 2, 1942
Deported to Auschwitz
September 10, 1944
Perished
The Jewish Museum, Prague
#133.420v

ANNE D. DUTLINGER

The artwork from Theresienstadt/Terezín, when shown in context with memoirs, essays, and documentary materials, reveals a complicated story. The exhibition, *The Arts as Strategies for Survival: Theresienstadt 1941–45*, and its two-day symposium, raised as many questions as it suggested answers about roles of art, music, and education in "Ghetto Theresienstadt." The purpose and result of artistic activities in Theresienstadt were as varied as the activities and personalities that produced them. Whether considered as documentary evidence, "spiritual resistance,"[2] or for its therapeutic benefits, the value of Theresienstadt's art is not restricted to draftsmanship or composition. An aesthetic judgment without consideration of conditions that shaped the making of art in Theresienstadt gives an incomplete account. The definition of survival is also problematic.

Did artistic activity sustain the spirit and promote survival in Theresienstadt? Self-control over process and its outcome, painfully absent in the lives of the inmates of the ghetto, could be momentarily achieved through creative work. A blank piece of paper provided a form of escape, access to memory and imagination, and a rare moment of privacy.

The artwork produced in Theresienstadt was, however, created in large part by those who would *not* survive. The work left by artists in Theresienstadt is all that remains of them—evidence of their talent, and a tragic symbol of lost potential. The art, music, and theater from Theresienstadt stands as an archive and memorial of the diverse and prolific cultural, artistic, and educational activities that took place there. But the quality and remarkable nature of the artists' achievements has also served to blur the truth. For most of its inmates, life in the "model ghetto" was only a temporary stop on the way to annihilation.[3]

Despite the inhumane, uncertain, and arbitrary living conditions in Theresienstadt, its artists produced a rich variety of work, which expressed and served different purposes. The works chosen for this exhibition do not separate self-expression from documentation, education from therapy, or entertainment from propaganda, but try to show how they existed together.

The heart of the exhibition, *The Arts as Strategies for Survival: Theresienstadt 1941–45*, was a selection of thirty original collages and paintings, produced by children of Theresienstadt in classes with their teacher, the Bauhaus artist Friedl Dicker-Brandeis. Artwork by Dicker-Brandeis, and other adult artists imprisoned in Theresienstadt —

Hanuš Klauber
Collage
Born January 24, 1929
Deported to Terezín
February 2, 1942
Deported to Auschwitz
September 10, 1944
Perished
*The Jewish Museum, Prague
#133.420r*

2

Marianna Rosenzweig
(Room 28)
Collage
Born May 5, 1930
Deported to Terezín
September 30, 1942
Deported to Auschwitz
September 10, 1944
Survived
The Jewish Museum, Prague
#133.056

including Norbert Troller, Josef Spier, Leo Haas, and scenic designs by František Zelenka—were included in the exhibition to illustrate the paradox of existence in the ghetto. Hunger, illness, and deportations were as much a part of daily life in Theresienstadt as were its cabaret, concerts, and lectures.[4]

The essays in this book were selected from papers presented at the symposium, *Art, Music and Education as Strategies for Survival: Theresienstadt 1941–45*, held at Moravian College on February 10–11, 2000, in conjunction with the opening of the exhibition.

"Art in the Context of Theresienstadt" by Sybil H. Milton explores the cultural life of "Ghetto Theresienstadt" within the context of the Final Solution. "Friedl Dicker-Brandeis: Lady in a Car," contributed by Michaela Hájková, Curator of the Graphics and Painting Collection at the Jewish Museum in Prague, deepens our understanding of this remarkable but underappreciated artist and teacher. Susan Leshnoff discusses Bauhaus pedagogy and Dicker-Brandeis's teaching methods in her essay, "Holocaust Survival and the Spirit of the Bauhaus." Rebecca Rovit, in "A Carousel of Theatrical Performances in Theresienstadt," examines cabaret, theater, and music produced in the Ghetto. Vojtěch Blodig's essay, "The Genocide of the Czech Jews in World War II and the Terezín Ghetto" reveals aspects of Theresienstadt's controversial reputation as a "rest home" for Jews privileged by class, military rank, intelligence, talent, or celebrity. In "Terezín Memorial: A Short History," Blodig relates how the former town of Terezín evolved into a memorial to the Holocaust, and its current role in the Czech Republic in Holocaust education.

Because it is difficult for students today, especially for young Americans, to connect to events that occurred before their lifetime, or beyond their borders, their initial confrontation with the Holocaust often raises the question, "But

how could anyone survive?" The exhibition at
Moravian College suggested possible answers
by combining survivors' testimonies, original
artwork, archival materials, and historical
research.

The personal histories of the survivors often reveal
accidents and ambiguities. Few survivors of
the Holocaust can tell one story, or name
one reason to answer, "How did you survive?"
Each survivor's history is unique, and most
are complicated. But many experiences by
survivors were shared, heard often in words
like "family," "faith," "friends," "health,"
"teachers," "talent," "luck," "music," "art,"
"theater. . . "

Memoirs by a group of survivors, "The Girls from
Room 28," students of Friedl Dicker-Brandeis,
provide personal examples of how art and
music sustained them in Theresienstadt.
The essay, "Coming of Age in Theresienstadt:
Friedl's Girls from Room 28," includes
extracts from interviews conducted by
Hannelore Wonschick with "the girls."
The full interviews will be published as a
memoir in the near future. The material is
introduced and edited by Anne D. Dutlinger.

Hindsight filters both what is remembered and
how we listen. Although fifty-five years have
passed since Theresienstadt was liberated,
"The Girls from Room 28," formerly children
in the ghetto, now grandmothers, have a
clear message to tell about the role of
art, music, and education as "strategies
for survival."

◄ *The Arts as Strategies for Survival:
Theresienstadt 1941–45* at
Payne Gallery of Moravian College,
Bethlehem, Pennsylvania

▼ A panel of survivors from
Theresienstadt at the symposium,
*Art, Music and Education as
Strategies for Survival:
Theresienstadt 1941–45*
l–r; Paul Aron Sandfort,
Ela Stein Weissberger,
Helga Weissová-Hosková
Photographs by Stephen M. Barth

The act of making art distills and gives structure to the complexity of experience: "...an act of portrayal...helps to clarify the structure of what is seen."[5] The exhibition at Moravian College, comprised of over two hundred works of art and artifacts from Theresien-stadt, could only suggest the full subject. The size of the collection in the Jewish Museum in Prague and the limited number of originals available for loan necessitated hard choices. Each drawing had a hand behind the pencil, with a unique style. "The children of Theresienstadt" quickly revealed their names, and individuality. Each competed for inclusion.

The work that most interested me as an artist and a teacher of design was not always what I chose to include for the exhibition. It would have been very easy, just from the collages produced by Theresienstadt's children, to create a "beautiful" exhibition. But I had concerns that an aesthetic approach was not only disrespectful but misleading. To establish Theresienstadt's sense of place and purpose required different choices. Content, in some cases, took precedence over form. In addition, I tried to give priority to work that had not been previously exhibited or published.

I was particularly interested in the collages. Similarities between the Theresienstadt children's "glue pictures,"[6] which used ledger paper, and the "ledger book drawings" by Plains Indians imprisoned in U.S. Army forts during the 1870s were striking. Through drawing, inmates of Theresienstadt, like the imprisioned warriors, interpreted the "...specifics of their condition. They could experiment with who they were becoming and they would, literally 'possessed by an image,' work through the trauma of the present and the recent past."[7] Despite profound differences between the two situations, in both, the transformation of bureaucratic forms into autobiographical art resonates as an act of self-affirmation. "To make a picture can be a revolutionary act, an act of covert resistance. It can be a way of mourning the past and fixing it in historical time as well."[8]

The ledger books, however, used for drawing by the imprisoned Native Americans, were also employed by their captors for recording numbers of prisoners and descriptions of appropriated possessions. In Theresienstadt, the ledger paper used by children for their collages was never intended for German record-keeping. Printed in Czech, the ledger paper in Theresienstadt was left over from when Terezín was a military training base for its own citizens, before German occupation. But use of the ledger paper, in both cases, adds its layer of language and meaning. How art can define and maintain identity is reflected in both the abstract portraits by children of Theresienstadt, and the in self-portraits by Native American prisoners as proud warriors.

The power of abstraction and the charm of directness generally admired in child art are seen in the artwork by Theresienstadt's children. But the context of their production shadows both interpretation and appreciation. Any reading of content or form is influenced by foreknowledge of the Holocaust. Familiar subjects of child art, like flowers, food, and trains, when drawn by the doomed children of Theresienstadt, can suggest entirely different meanings and gain heightened symbolic importance.

The study or analysis of the child art from Theresienstadt, whether in terms of form, content, or pyschological meaning, is not the intention of this book. As the exhibition and this book show, many inmates of Theresienstadt maintained the will to live through human connections and creative work. The mental and physical engagement required to create art, play music, or perform theater were "strategies for survival." Art and music provided a way to forget and remember, to believe in and imagine the other world—the familiar, reassuring world of home. The range, amount, and quality of art produced in Theresienstadt remains as impressive, poignant evidence of its artists' determination, talent, and potential.

The ledger paper used in the collage was for monthly deposits to a bank, i.e., *lednu* is Czech for "January."

Helena Mändl
(Room 28)
Collage
Born May 21, 1930
Deported to Terezín
December 17, 1943
Deported to Auschwitz
December 18, 1943
Perished
The Jewish Museum, Prague #121.586

6

Eva Kohn (Room 28)
Collage
Born July 8, 1930
Deported to Terezín
September 9, 1942
Perished
The Jewish Museum, Prague
#125.721

Many examples of child art from Theresienstadt show clear evidence of Bauhaus pedagogy, passed down to them by their teacher, Friedl Dicker-Brandeis.[9] Influences on Dicker-Brandeis present a remarkable cross-fertilization of early twentieth-century ideas about art, art education, and political activism. Her mentors and teachers included Franz Čížek, Johannes Itten, Walter Gropius, Paul Klee and Vasily Kandinsky. Dicker-Brandeis's legacy, contained in her art and that of her young students, is a compelling portrait of an altruistic life dedicated to art and teaching.[10]

Her life reflects a fascinating combination of influences. Dicker-Brandeis's teaching reveals Čížek's belief in the unique value and quality of child art—"There is an art that children make for themselves. . . . to make real his own desires, inclinations and dreams. . . . We have no art that it so direct as that of children."[11] Franz Čížek's lasting influence on art education was his principle of supportive nonintervention as the foundation of creativity and self-expression.[12]

Čížek's teaching method of undirected self-expression and the disciplined, utopian pedagogy of the Bauhaus formed the teaching philosophies of Friedl Dicker-Brandeis. As a student and instructor at the Bauhaus, Dicker-Brandeis was also aware of Klee and Kandinsky's interest in and use

Jana Pollack
Pencil on paper
Born January 23, 1932
Deported to Terezín
July 5, 1943
Deported to Auschwitz
October 4, 1944
Survived
The Jewish Museum, Prague
#133.0101

of child art.[13] Teaching methods developed by Dicker-Brandeis in Theresienstadt blended Bauhaus projects, guided exercises, and creative freedom.[14]

While art creates "a belief in an internal, rather than external, sense of control of one's life,"[15] the benefit of art as a tool for coping, as a "strategy for survival," was no assurance or guarantee of survival in Theresienstadt. Any individual satisfaction from artistic endeavor was brief, most likely limited to the time of its production. No piece of artwork or its signature, no performance, text or composition was lasting protection against orders onto a transport to "the East."

Surviving one more day to live out the next was no small achievement in Theresienstadt. But individual identity could be reclaimed—albeit momentarily—through art. Art, music, and performance transformed fear into

freedom. The act of making art suspended the collective nightmare, and replaced the arbitrary rules of the ghetto with individual purpose. It helped to sustain hope, a sense of the self, and the will to live.

The theory that art can heal trauma evolved, in part, from the work of a student of Friedl Dicker-Brandeis, Edith Kramer. In *Art as Therapy with Children*, (dedicated by Kramer to Friedl) Kramer describes "art as therapy" as "a means of supporting the ego, fostering the development of a sense of identity, and promoting maturation.... Its main function is seen in the power of art to contribute to the development of psychic organization that is able to function under pressure without breakdown...."[16] Prior to emigrating to the United States with her family, Kramer attended art classes that Dicker-Brandeis held for children of Jewish refugees in Prague.[17]

The power of art to express and heal the spirit is defined in different ways by the selected essays presented here. Despite a rich exchange of ideas from the presentations given at the symposium, limited space, unfortunately, did not allow all of them to

Lea Pollack
Pencil on paper
Born March 21, 1930
Deported to Terezín
December 12, 1942
Deported to Auschwitz
May 18, 1944
Perished
The Jewish Museum, Prague
#131.712r

8

be included in this book. I hope the interest generated by the symposium and exhibition will result in the publication of the remaining essays. Titles of the essays and a list of symposium participants begins on page 194.

Text panels written for the exhibition appear throughout this book as sidebars adjacent to or following relevant essays. All text panels were written by Sybil H. Milton, except for those which appear in "A Carousel of Theatrical Performance in Theresienstadt," which were provided by its author, Rebecca Rovit.

Developed for propaganda purposes by the Germans, Theresienstadt, the "model ghetto," evolved into a complex and well-designed set piece, seemingly populated by actively engaged artists and musicians, intellectuals, civic leaders, and children at play. Scenes of concerts and cabarets at Theresienstadt masked its existence as "the Gateway to Auschwitz." Hitler's goal to rid German-occupied territories of anyone outside his evolving definition of racial purity and social acceptability was well served by the appearances projected by Theresienstadt."[18]

The skewed, stage-set entrance to our exhibition, seen on the title page of this book, suggested the paradox of life in Theresienstadt. The arched passage into the gallery, overlaid by burned train tracks, was inspired by ink sketches done in Theresienstadt by Bedřich Fritta. The portal and display panels were designed by Timothy Averill.

The artwork created by the children and adults in Theresienstadt was in large part preserved, although most of their creators perished. An estimated 1,000 children from Theresienstadt survived. The rest, with their parents, teachers, and friends, vanished into trains. Most were killed in the gas chambers at Auschwitz-Birkenau.

The child art hidden by Friedl Dicker-Brandeis, was carried out of the ghetto after liberation in two suitcases by Willy Groag, a leader of one of the childrens' homes.[19] The art he rescued has now gained relative fame. The drawings hold a significant place both as art and evidence, as well as a tool for teaching. The optimism and innocence revealed in much of the child art ironically provides access to the darker truth of their victimization. This art endures as a memorial to its young makers and to their teacher, Friedl Dicker-Brandeis. It also provides a window into the illusion and reality of life in "Ghetto Theresienstadt."

NOTES

1. Helga Weissová, *Zeichne, was Du siehst: Zeichnungen eines Kindes aus Theresienstadt/Terezín* (Göttingen, 1998), 120.

2. Union of Hebrew Congregations, *Spiritual Resistance: Art from Concentration Camps* (New York, 1978).

3. Miroslav Karny, "The Genocide of the Czech Jews," in *Terezín Memorial Book: Jewish Victims of Nazi Deportations from Bohemia and Moravia* (Prague, 1996), 47–55.

4. Gerald Green, *The Artists of Terezín* (New York, 1989), 51.

5. Rudolph Arnheim, "Beginning with the Child," in *Discovering Child Art: Essays on Childhood, Primitivism and Modernism,* ed. Jonathan Fineberg (Princeton, 1998), 16.

6. Barbara Wörwag, "'There is an Unconscious, Vast Power in the Child': Notes on Kandinsky, Münter and Children's Drawings," in *Discovering Child Art*, 71. See also Franz Čížek, *Children's Colored Paper Work* (Vienna, 1927), 9–14.

7. Anna Blume, "In Place of Writing," in *Plains Indians Drawings 1865–1935: Pages from a Visual History* (New York, 1996), 40.

8. Janet Catherine Berlo, "Drawing and Being Drawn In: The Late-Nineteenth-Century Plains Graphic Artist and the Intercultural Encounter," in *Plains Indians Drawings 1865–1935: Pages from a Visual History,* eds. Janet Catherine Berlo et al. (New York, 1996), 18.

9. Elena Makarova, *From Bauhaus to Terezín: Friedl Dicker-Brandeis and Her Pupils* (Jerusalem, 1990), 4–35.

10. Ibid.

11. Wilhelm Viola, *Child Art and Franz Čížek* (Vienna, 1936), 34–35.

12. Cathy A. Malchiodi, *Understanding Children's Drawings* (New York 1998), 126.

13. Jonathan Fineberg, *The Innocent Eye: Children's Art and the Modern Artist* (Princeton, 1997), 49. "In the 1920s at the Bauhaus Kandinsky began collecting children's drawings again in tandem with his close friend Klee." See also Fineberg's discussion of exhibitions of child art, which began in the 1890s, 11–16. "Artists were increasingly involved in organizing the

Hanna Brady (Room 28)
Gouache
Born May 16, 1929
Deported to Terezín
May 18, 1942
Deported to Auschwitz
October 23, 1944
Perished
The Jewish Museum, Prague
#131.710

number of exhibitions of child art after the turn of the century while at the same time looking ever more closely at various aspects of how children drew as a stimulus to their own work....Expressionists, cubists, futurists and artists of the avante-garde Russian movements all hung the art of children alongside their own... the first room of the 1908 Vienna 'Kunstschau' (in which Oscar Kokoschka debuted) was an exhibition of children's art from the classes of Franz Čížek." 12

14. Makarova, *From Bauhaus to Terezín*, 30–35.

15. Malchiodi, 158.

16. Edith Kramer, *Art as Therapy with Children* (New York, 1971), xiii.

17. Ibid., xiv.

18. Karny, 47–55.

19. Makarova, *From Bauhaus to Terezín* (Jerusalem, 1990), 24.

▲ Unknown Photographer
  Aerial view of the Theresienstadt
  Small Fortress and national cemetery,
  photographed after liberation, 1945
  Czechoslovak News Agency, Prague

▶ Otto Ungar
  Children Playing in Theresienstadt
  gouache, n.d.
  *Simon Wiesenthal
  Museum of Tolerance, Los Angeles*

SYBIL H. MILTON

THE SETTING AND THE MYTH

In late 1941, the SS converted Theresienstadt (Terezín) into a ghetto.[1] The so-called "model ghetto" of Theresienstadt, an eighteenth-century walled Austrian garrison town in Bohemia located about forty miles northwest of Prague, was the only Jewish ghetto in Nazi-occupied Europe that was located in an area where there had been no previous Jewish presence. Unlike other ghettos created by the Nazi regime, Theresienstadt was not a sealed section of a town or city.

Arranged in a simple geometric street grid, the town was approximately two-thirds of a mile long and wide, containing about two hundred two-storied houses and fourteen large stone barracks. These barracks served as dormitories for communal living and also contained offices, workshops, infirmaries, and kitchens. The fortifications formed a ten-pointed star with walls, moats, and bulwarks around the symmetrical town. This small town included six avenues and nine streets with a parade square at the center. The Austrian garrison town was converted for civilian use in 1882 and had a population of approximately 7,000 at the time the Germans cleared it to construct the ghetto. The town also included a church, a tavern, a school, administrative buildings, and a town square. The loose double ring of baroque fortifications not only sealed off the ghetto, but also enabled the SS easily to control the prisoners.

▶ Unknown Photographer
Prisoners entering gate "Arbeit Macht Frei" ("Labor Liberates") at the Small Fortress in Theresienstadt, 1943–44
Bildarchiv Preussischer Kulturbesitz, Berlin

▼ Photograph by James Hauser
Small Fortress, Terezín, 1999

Three gates, protected by the fortifications, were the only entrances. Furthermore, the adjacent Little Fortress, located across the Ohre river (Eger river in German), previously a military prison, was ideal for similar use by the Gestapo, since it was already equipped with solitary confinement cells, gallows, and a plaza for firing squads.[2]

DEPORTATION AND ARRIVAL IN THERESIENSTADT

By late 1941, systematic deportations from Germany to the East had begun. During 1942 and 1943, many of the deportation trains from Germany, Austria, Holland, and even Denmark traveled to Theresienstadt. When notified of their "resettlement," an euphemism for forced deportation, Jews received specific instructions. The SS and police made it clear to all deportees that failure to adhere to these instructions would mean immediate prosecution or death. These rigid and precise orders included instructions to pack 50 kilograms (ca. 110 pounds) of possessions to take with them.

In many cases, Jews had been given specific lists of items to pack. These included a bedroll, blankets, underwear, shirts, slacks, shoes, boots, sweaters, coats, and household utensils, such as pots, bowls, tea strainers, forks, and spoons.

For the deportees, these packing instructions created an illusion of survival and enabled the SS and native police to control large numbers of deportees being deported to Theresienstadt and other localities in the East. The deportees could not know that their choices in packing might later be critical for survival: an extra pair of warm socks might mean the difference between exposure and survival.

For an artist, paper and a small block of primary watercolors could mean the ability to record and document what one experienced.

In normal times, suitcases are associated with travel, either for business or pleasure. Within the context of the Holocaust, these suitcases symbolized the German manipulation of the deportees' hopes for survival as well as a subterfuge enabling them to enforce crowd control; for the victims, they represented the immense human tragedy of dislocation, and of involuntarily loss of family and community alongside the abandonment of homes and possessions.

Unknown Photographer
Transport from Bauschowitz (Bohusoviče).
Note work crew and local residents on the
right side of the street, n.d.
The Jewish Museum, Prague
Fotoarchiv #23.938

12

On October 10, 1941, Reinhard Heydrich, Adolf Eichmann, and other high-ranking Nazi officials selected Terezín, from among some twenty Bohemian towns, to be converted into a ghetto for Jewish deportees en route to the killing centers of the East. Terezín was chosen for pragmatic reasons, as the small town population could easily be resettled and the costs covered by the sale of abandoned and confiscated Jewish property.

The Theresienstadt ghetto differed from all other ghettos. It was designed to deceive the outside world and to hide the truth of the murder of the Jews from public opinion. Theresienstadt opened in December 1941 and at first served as a transit camp for Czech Jews from the Protectorate before they were deported to the East in the winter of 1941–42. Starting in June 1942, transports of Jews from Germany and Austria arrived. These included the elderly as well as decorated and disabled veterans of the First World War, prominent Jews with special connections, and persons in mixed marriages with non-Jewish spouses or parents and their children. The use of Theresienstadt as a way station for elderly German and Austrian Jews in transit to the East served to hide the radical nature of these deportations from the public. Here we can see the roots of the deadly deception that would establish the postwar

◄ Unknown Photographer
Deportation of Czech Jews from Pilsen (Plžen) to Bauschowitz (Bohusoviče) accompanied by SS guards, 1941–44
The Jewish Museum, Prague Fotoarchiv #21.728/1

◄ Unknown Photographer
Arrival of Dutch Jews in Theresienstadt, April 1943
Bildarchiv Preussischer Kulturbesitz, Berlin

notoriety of Theresienstadt as the symbol for Nazi duplicity.[3]

The Theresienstadt "Old Age" Ghetto deception did, however, pose some technical problems involving the confiscation of the assets and properties of the deported Jews. The first deportations of German Jews to the East—those to Lodz in October 1941—relied on a 1933 law about the confiscation of

14

Ivan Vojtěch Fric

Fric was one of two Czech
non-prisoner cameramen
employed by the Prague
newsreel company Aktualita
to make the 1944 propaganda
film. He began filming the
arrival of Dutch transports
into the ghetto on January 20,
1944.

Arriving Jewish transport
from the Netherlands in
Theresienstadt; deportees
carry their belongings to a
ghetto entrance. The train
tracks from Bauschowitz
(Bohusoviče) to the ghetto
are visible. The photograph
was probably taken on January
18 or February 25, 1944.

United States Holocaust
Memorial Museum
w/s #20255

Transport of Dutch Jews arrives in
Theresienstadt carrying their bed-rolls and
hand luggage as they enter the central
courtyard, or *schleuse*,
February 1944
*United States Holocaust Memorial Museum
w/s #20273*

15

"subversive property."[4] This involved a
cumbersome procedure and was thus
replaced in late November 1941 by the well-
known Eleventh Ordinance to the Reich
Citizenship Law. But this simple solution
applied only to deportations across the
borders of the Reich, and thus could not be
applied to the property of Jews sent to
Theresienstadt. Because Theresienstadt was
located in the Protectorate of Bohemia and
Moravia, and thus within the borders of the
German Reich, the provisions of the Eleventh
decree did not apply. To obtain the property
of these elderly German and Austrian Jews,
the Central Office for Reich Security invented
the notorious *Heimeinkaufverträge*.[5] This
devious solution was another elaborate
deception of the deportees, since it imitated
the method used to buy places in nursing
homes, forcing the elderly to sign contracts
relinquishing their remaining property in
exchange for perpetual care. This hoax
resulted in vast sums of money going to the
coffers of the Central Office for Reich
Security. In fact, the Gestapo cynically called
these deportations to Theresienstadt a
"change of address" (*Wohnsitzverlegung*).

These plans formulated in late 1941 were imple-
mented in 1942 and determined the future
of Theresienstadt. More than 140,000
European Jews, 74,000 of them from
Bohemia and Moravia, were incarcerated
in Theresienstadt. Deportations of

Ivan Vojtěch Fric
Transport of Dutch Jews wait in
the *schleuse* with their bed-rolls
and luggage, February 1944
*United States Holocaust
Memorial Museum w/s #20267*

Unknown Photographer
The Transport Information
Department in Prague, n.d.
The Jewish Museum, Prague
#22.070/2

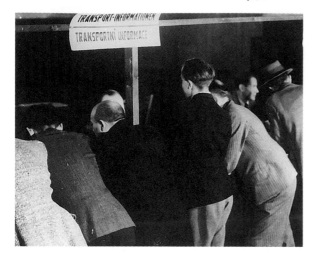

DEPORTATION AND ARRIVAL IN THERESIENSTADT

After reporting to designated assembly centers, as many deportees as possible were jammed into trains as if they were freight. The trip to Theresienstadt usually lasted about two days or less. The transports were overcrowded and conditions often unsanitary. Deportees usually had to subsist on the food they had brought with them, and by the time they reached their destination, all food and drink had long been consumed.

The process of deportation and the instructions for these transports reveal the systematic pattern of Nazi deceptions that continued in the "model ghetto."

New arrivals at Theresienstadt, usually loaded down with suitcases, bundles, rucksacks, bedrolls, and even cooking utensils, were forced to spend one or two days in the *schleuse* (channel or funnel).

There the deportees were registered and their luggage searched, sorted, and systematically robbed of many of their last possessions. The arriving prisoners were given a few tubs with soup, potatoes, and bread. Every new arrival passed through the *schleuse* in Theresienstadt.

approximately 43,000 German and 15,000 Austrian Jews commenced in June 1942. Between late April 1943 and early September 1944, about 4,570 Dutch Jews (including German Jewish refugees and those in mixed marriages) and in early October 1943, about 400 Danish Jews were also transported to Theresienstadt; for these Jews from the Low countries and Scandanavia, Theresienstadt was an alternative option to the deception of the early Bergen-Belsen exchange camp. [6]

Approximately 35,000 deportees died in the Theresienstadt ghetto, but the majority of deportees, about 88,000, were redeported from Theresienstadt to their death in the East. The transports leaving Theresienstadt for the East followed the general pattern of deportations from the Reich. [7] Also about 1,200 Polish children from the liquidated Bialystok ghetto were brought to Theresienstadt and segregated there from most other prisoners for about five weeks from late August to early October 1943, before they were deported to Auschwitz-Birkenau. [8]

During the last phase of the war after December 1944, approximately 14,000 concentration camp prisoners from eastern camps were dumped into Theresienstadt. This included Slovakian Jews from the Sered labor and internment camp, German and Czech Jews in mixed marriages and previously protected

Unknown Photographer
Loading horse-drawn carts with
luggage of Jewish deportees.
The photograph is probably
a deportation from There-
sienstadt to Pilsen, (Plžen)
and the East in 1942.
The Jewish Museum, Prague
#20.505

 SS Photographer

Jewish women and children from the town of Bilke, Bereg county via Berehovo (Beregszász),
arriving on the ramp at Auschwitz-Birkenau on a transport from Subcarpathian Ruthenia in early
summer 1944. Subcarpathian Ruthenia was a region that the Germans had transferred from Czech
to Hungarian control in March 1939, and today is in the Ukraine.

After the German occupation of Hungary in March 1944, deportations to Auschwitz-Birkenau
began from this region in mid-April and May. This photographed is reproduced in *Auschwitz Album*
(New York, 1981), from an album located after liberation by Lili Jacob Zelmanovic (Meier), which
includes photographs of her family's arrival at Auschwitz-Birkenau.

At the far left is her aunt Tauba with her five children and her mother's sister Rywka with her two
children (with white hats).

Yad Vashem, Copy courtesy The Jewish Museum, Prague #2.288

Unknown Photographer
Jewish workers preparing
an inventory of confiscated property.
More than forty-five warehouses in
Prague amassed confiscated goods,
including household and office
furniture, pianos and instruments,
machines, fine art, cultural property,
and ceremonial objects., n.d.
The Jewish Museum, Prague #3.738

18

Ivan Vojtěch Fric

Dutch Jews deported to Theresienstadt on a ghetto street; a teenage girl carries two small pots on a street in the ghetto. All pedestrians are wearing stars. The two women on the sidewalk (on the left) have obviously lost weight since their clothing is loose, February 1944

United States Holocaust Memorial Museum w/s #20259

Ivan Vojtěch Fric

Transport of Dutch Jews arrive in Theresienstadt and receive their first meal, 1944

United States Holocaust Memorial Museum w/s #20257

part-Jews (*Mischlinge*), and about 1,150 Hungarian Jews.[9] The Soviet Army liberated the remaining Theresienstadt prisoners on May 8, 1945.

The Theresienstadt ghetto was thus, as we now know, a camp designed as a link in the chain that inevitably led to the gas chambers and also an elaborate hoax to deceive international opinion. As part of this deception, the SS tolerated some cultural activities, including theater, music, lectures, and concerts. Other cultural activities, such as art and teaching the children were not specifically prohibited, but carried risks if discovered.

But while we now know that Terezín was nothing but a way-station to the killing centers, the posthumous fame of Theresienstadt is based primarily on the myth created by this hoax. This mythology includes children's poetry and drawings, artwork by adults, lectures and cultural programs (euphemistically called *Freizeitgestaltung* or "leisure time activities"), soccer games, and the well-known Nazi movie production. And while we know that this was not the reality of Terezín, the reason for continued international interest remains the mythology the hoax created.

Josef Spier, *The Aryan Way*
Watercolor and ink on paper, n.d.
Leo Baeck Institute, New York

ART AND THE MYTH OF THERESIENSTADT

The pathos and haunting beauty of Terezín art is disconcerting, since the artists were themselves pawns and victims of the Nazis. Art and culture served as a psychological escape from confinement, enabling the victims to regain some control of their own personal space and time. Nevertheless, this art has provided a pretext for the postwar legend that conditions in Theresienstadt were not as bad as the Polish ghettos, since the profusion of cultural activities has been misinterpreted as alleviating the harsh conditions of daily life. Although the similarity and simultaneity of various clandestine ghetto archives as a conscious form of spiritual resistance and documentation is seldom mentioned in postwar scholarship, it is nevertheless clear that Theresienstadt art, hidden in the walls and attics of ghetto buildings, paralleled the scope of Emanuel Ringelblum's underground Oneg Shabbat archive in Warsaw.[10]

Similarly the documentary validity of this Terezín art has been dismissed by many scholars because of the mistaken belief that aesthetic considerations automatically distorted the factual accuracy of its contents, whereas art museums have ignored and dismissed this art as aesthetically marginal and of transient significance.[11] The mythology of Terezín art and cultural life has thus served to obscure the significance and place of Theresienstadt in the "Final Solution."

The function of art at Theresienstadt was complex. It is obviously disconcerting to us today that conditions that barely sustained life resulted in the creation of artistic works: plastic arts, literature, music, and theater. The relationship between a flourishing clandestine culture and the brutality of the milieu in which it was produced has led to two misconceptions: 1) a pragmatic fear that art could be used as an alibi minimizing the horrors, and 2) a simplistic and vague identification of works of art with "spiritual resistance." The relationship between arts and atrocity, although not yet fully understood, enriches our understanding of the special place of Theresienstadt in the Nazi ghetto and camp system, and at the time, enabled artists to retain their individuality and survive under conditions of extreme duress.

Art, whether clandestine or commissioned, served diverse functions at Theresienstadt: documentation, decoration, catharsis, and survival. Art from Theresienstadt does not refer to a single school, generation, or national style of art, but only to the location where this art was made between 1941 and 1945. It was done by professional artists as well as amateurs and children. Artwork was a labor detail for professionally trained

...I look, I look
      into the wide world,
           into the wide distant world.
I look to the southeast,
      I look, I look toward my home....

Franta Bass, 1944
extract from "Home," in Hana Volavková, ed.,
...I never saw another butterfly... Children's Drawings and Poems from Terezín Concentration Camp 1942–1944,
(New York, 1993), 10

Sona Waldstein
Watercolor on paper
Born November 28, 1926
Deported to Terezín
March 6, 1943
Perished
*The Jewish Musem, Prague
#131.770*

Ruth Weiss
Pastel and pencil on paper
Born March 16, 1931
Deported to Terezín November 20, 1942
Deported to Auschwitz May 18, 1944
Perished

The Jewish Museum, Prague
#133.238

Edita Fischl
Pencil and watercolor
Born March 30, 1932
Deported to Terezín
September 8, 1942
Survived
The Jewish Museum, Prague
#131.836

Unknown Child Artist
Pencil on paper, n.d.
The Jewish Museum, Prague
#133.010v

painters, sculptors, architects, and draftsmen assigned to the Technical Department of the Jewish ghetto administration. Many artists also worked at the Lautsch company workshops in Theresienstadt between March 1942 and September 1943 producing decorative objects, ceramics, novelties, copies of old masters, and other paintings.[12] Artists were also assigned to create stage sets and designs for theater productions, to produce sketches for the 1944 Nazi propaganda film popularly known today as *The Führer Gives a Town to the Jews* but actually entitled *Theresienstadt: A Documentary Film from the Jewish Settlement Area.*[13]

Materials available for officially commissioned works thus provided supplies for secret sketches, portraits, and caricatures. Thus official labor assignments enabled the artists to obtain access to paper, canvas, oil, and other supplies for their clandestine art. Occasionally such labor afforded them better rations for themselves and others, sometimes by trading small craft objects for food on the black market that existed in every camp and ghetto.

Milan (Marvan) Eisler
Pencil on paper
Born July 29, 1932
Deported to Terezín
June 13, 1942
Survived
The Jewish Museum, Prague
#131.762

PORTRAITS: MIRRORS OF MEMORY

The largest single group of Holocaust art by children and adults were portraits. Diaries and documents attest to the fact that this was the most common genre. Portraits had a magical meaning during the Holocaust (and also in many native and folk art forms). They gave the subject a sense of permanent presence among the living, extremely important when temporal physical presence was so fragile and tenuous.

The depiction of one's own or another person's likeness, without abstraction or symbolization, was a cohesive metaphor for the value of individual life juxtaposed to the mass terror of the Holocaust. All art functions as a bond and common language, and portraits, in particular, created a means of communication and a sense of community among the victims as well as a language of visual communication between ghetto inhabitants.

Sometimes portraits were countersigned by both artist and sitter. Women artists seem to have painted a substantially larger number of children's portraits and collective scenes in camp infirmaries, showing small groups of women helping each other. These thematic distinctions are not accidental. Recent research about gender specific aspects of the Holocaust indicate that art reflects reality; thus, mothers and small children were usually placed together during the deportations and selections, and women were usually assigned to care for those children who survived in the camps and ghettos.

Occasionally, portraits would also be commissioned by the Germans as gifts to superiors or to their own families. If the resulting work was acceptable, it often helped secure more lenient work assignments or better rations.

Norbert Troller
Accordion
Pencil on paper
Theresienstadt, 1942
*Estate of the artist, Doris Rauch; Troller
Collection, Leo Baeck Institute, New York*

Art at Theresienstadt also had an administrative function for illustrating official reports, designing camp signage, and posters; it was also utilized in official propaganda. Obviously compulsory work produced by inmate artists was meticulously executed and technically excellent, since the interned artists' fate depended on compliance with German orders. Moreover, paper, ink, and watercolor available through official work could—with luck—be siphoned off as supplies for clandestine art.

Initially, some of the incarcerated artists had also brought art supplies with them. For example, Charlotta Burešová brought supplies from the remains of her Prague art studio to Theresienstadt. Burešová periodically received additional items in food parcels from her husband. Otto Ungar, after receiving his notice for deportation in Brno in January 1942, packed more art supplies than food in his suitcase. It is remarkable that artists made the effort to carry such supplies with them, since official limitations on the quantity of personal belongings meant that for every sketch pad packed into one small suitcase, something of vital importance had to be left behind.

Otto Ungar

Karel Fleischmann

Petr Kien

Rafael Schächter

*Dicker-Brandeis, Copy courtesy The Jewish Museum, Prague
Ungar, Fleischmann, Kien and Schächter, Courtesy of Terezín Memorial*

Individual stylistic preference and the skill and personality of the artist were obvious determinants of the character of the artistic product. Clandestine artists always chose what subject they depicted and also the materials that they used, however limited in availability. Artists usually could not work openly, nor could they exhibit in galleries and museums. It must be remembered that restrictions placed on incarcerated artists in Theresienstadt and other sites of the Holocaust constituted arbitrary limitations on their creative possibilities. Nevertheless, many of the incarcerated artists simultaneously sketched the same scene both as clandestine and as "officially" commissioned art, enabling us to understand the ambivalent realities of ghetto life.

Although there is no definitive statistical data about the number of professional artists incarcerated in Theresienstadt, we can state with certainty that there were more than thirty-four German, Austrian, Dutch, and Czech professional artists and architects incarcerated at various times. [14] We know, for example, that more than twenty Jewish artists had been deported from the Theresienstadt ghetto to Auschwitz-Birkenau between late 1943 and late 1944. These included five Czech artists involved in the so-called "painter's affair of 1944," i.e., Leo Haas, Norbert Troller, Otto Ungar, Bedřich Fritta (pseudonym for Fritz Taussig), and Ferdinand Bloch. [15] The unusual richness in clandestine art possible at Theresienstadt was not feasible at Auschwitz-Birkenau and most other camps and ghettos.

Most of the Theresienstadt deportees, including the artists, were subsequently killed at the Auschwitz-Birkenau killing center, including František Zelenka, who had designed the sets and produced the children's opera *Brundibár* at Theresienstadt, the physician and artist Karel Fleischmann, and Petr Kien, who had served as deputy director of the Drawing Office of the Technical Department at Theresienstadt. The work of professional and amateur adult artists is obviously connected to the children's art at Theresienstadt.

Alice Sittig (Room 28)
Collage
Born April 19, 1930
Deported to Terezín
April 19, 1942
Deported to Auschwitz
May 18, 1944
Perished
The Jewish Museum, Prague
#133.475r

CHILDREN'S ART AT THERESIENSTADT

Perhaps the most unusual aspect of Theresienstadt is the story of its children. It is
estimated that possibly as many as 12,000
children under the age of eighteen had been
deported to Theresienstadt; about 1,560 of
them below the age of fifteen or who had
reached the age of fifteen in Theresienstadt
survived at liberation.[16]

Of course, it is impossible to conceptualize
children as a single group, because of the
enormous and complex variations in their
backgrounds and the distinct needs of three
different age groups ranging from infants to
adolescents. Even the word "children" is an
umbrella concept that includes at least three
distinct subgroups: 1) infants and toddlers up
to the age of six; 2) young children ages
seven to twelve; and 3) adolescents from
fourteen to seventeen years old. Their
respective chances for survival and their
ability to perform physical labor varied
enormously by age. Chances of survival were
somewhat higher for older children and
adolescents, since they could potentially be
assigned to and survive forced labor.

It must also be stated explicitly that children as
such were seldom the targets or victims of
Nazi violence because they were children.
They were persecuted along with their
families for racial, religious, or political
reasons. Nazi arrests and deportations had
been directed against all members of Jewish

Egon Seidel
Watercolor
Born July 2, 1931
Deported to Terezín
March 8, 1943
Deported to Auschwitz
October 19, 1944
Perished

The Jewish Museum, Prague
#131.522

The signs on this photograph translated from top to bottom specify:

"No access for Jews"

"Children's playground of the central welfare office of the capital city of Prague"

"This playground may be used by youngsters up to the age of fourteen. Adults are allowed entry only if accompanying children."

"Do not make your playground filthy; do not damage trees, shrubs, or playground equipment. Soccer is prohibited in this playground."

The heading of the fifth sign addressed to "those accompanying children" is only partly readable.

28

Unknown Photographer
Children's playground at
Charles Square (Karlovo Náměstí)
in Prague with signs in German
and Czech prohibiting Jews, 1939
Bildarchiv Preussischer Kulturbesitz, Berlin

families, without concern for age; this was also often the case with Gypsy families.

Few younger children understood why they were there or why they had previously been expelled from their schools and homes, forced to wear yellow stars on their clothing, and allowed to play only in designated restricted areas. Most of the children in Theresienstadt were forced to live in barracks separated from their parents; conditions were overcrowded, unsanitary, and sometimes posed the risks of epidemics and disease. There was no freedom, hunger and fear were always present. Children above the age of twelve were required to work.

Children's activities in Theresienstadt were administered by Jewish adults who saw to it that the children received slightly better food rations and housing conditions. Great sacrifices were made by adults to care for the young. Although teaching was not specifically forbidden by the Nazis, it was also not explicitly allowed; thus, school classes were conducted in semi-tolerated secrecy. Older prisoners taught the children most basic subjects, so that they would not be illiterate. Orphans were often adopted by families in the ghetto. A youth welfare service (*Jugendfürsorge*) set up schedules for leisure time, including daily educational play sessions, competitive sports, readings of poetry and drama, and theatrical or musical performances.[17]

Teaching was both formal and informal. Language instruction in Czech and Hebrew, literature, music, and history was usually conducted in the evenings after work hours and on Saturday mornings. The curriculum in these homes blended German and Czech progressive education with Zionism, socialism, and communism and provided youngsters with a basic education in art, literature, the humanities, and social science. Science was more difficult to teach, but biology was often explained through animals (butterflies, mice, lice, etc.) and trees or plants found or grown in the ghetto. Informal instruction consisted of participation and/or attendance at lectures, concerts, and theater performances.

In numerous acts of spiritual resistance, the adults responded to the collapse of their own world by attempting to create as normal a world as possible for the children.[18] In the clandestine schools, there was a relatively large degree of pedagogical freedom, despite—and paradoxically perhaps because of—ghetto conditions. Teachers could usually establish their curricula without outside interference.

Art was considered especially important as a form of psychological release or therapy, and also for the transmission of a cultural and religious heritage, and thus it became a form of resistance and education for survival. Art served to express emotions, memories, and experiences that had to be shaped into a

◄ Jiri Beutler
Pencil on paper
Born March 9, 1932
Deported to Terezín
September 19, 1942
Deported to Auschwitz
May 5, 1944
Perished
The Jewish Museum, Prague
#125.426

▼ Eva Wertheimstein
Pastel and pencil on paper
Born June 18, 1933
Deported to Terezín
December 5, 1941
Deported to Auschwitz
October 4, 1944
Perished

The Jewish Museum, Prague
#131.673

symbolic language, irrespective of the age or degree of skill of the child artists. Often art was based an assigned themes as well as freely chosen subjects.[19]

Teachers held special places as role models and surrogate parents. They understood how to forge a bond with the children and to motivate them to express their experiences in the symbolic language of art. Progressive teachers like Friedl Dicker-Brandeis in art[20] and Fredy Hirsch in sports[21] facilitated education for life. The children painted and drew freely, using art as an outlet for their imagination as well as an escape, enabling them to gain control of their own personal space and time.

Although very little is known about most of the children as individuals, many of them lived in eleven collective children's homes, such as L410 for Czech girls ages eight to sixteen, where Friedl Dicker-Brandeis lived and taught art. She also held an exhibition of children's art in the cellar of L410 in mid-July 1943.[22] The home L417, formerly a school, was used for Czech boys ages ten to fifteen.

There the weekly magazine *Vedem* ("We Lead") was produced from mid-December 1942 to August 1944, and the teenagers created their own nation, known as the "Republic of Shkid." Shkid was an acronym for the Russian phrase *shkolá iměni Dostoyevskovo* [Dostoyevsky School], a school for orphans in post-1918 St. Petersburg.[23] The use of the acronym "Shkid" united the children in their own "secret" community with their own rituals and symbols.

Other periodicals included *Bonaco*, an acronym which in Czech meant "a disorderly brothel," produced by girls residing in L414, housing German and Czech girls ages ten to fourteen in separate units. Home L417 produced the journal *Rim, Rim, Rim*, an alliterative sequence for the Hebrew word *netzarim* meaning "offspring" or "sprout."[24] These periodicals routinely included illustrations and art work by the child authors.

Edita Fischl
Colored pencil on paper
Born March 30, 1932
Deported to Terezín
September 8, 1942
Survived

The Jewish Museum, Prague
#131.799

Milan (Marvan) Eisler
Pencil on paper
Born July 29, 1932
Deported to Terezín
June 13, 1942
Survived

The Jewish Museum, Prague
#133.028

Milan (Marvan) Eisler
Pencil on paper
Born July 29, 1932
Deported to Terezín
June 13, 1942
Survived

The Jewish Museum, Prague
#133.041

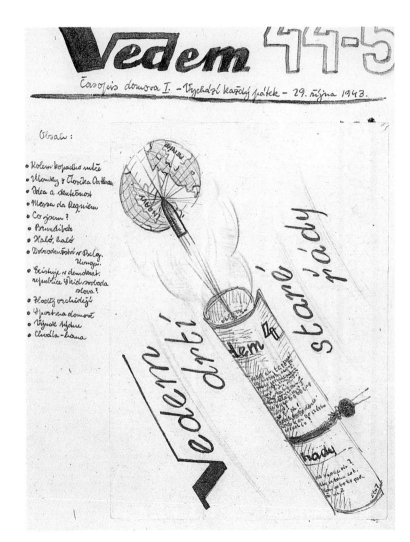

Vedem, "We Lead"
Magazine cover
Issue nos. 44–45, 1943
Terezín Memorial

Helga Weissová-Hosková
The Dormitory in the Barracks
Watercolor and ink, 1942
*Wallstein Verlag, Göttingen,
Germany*

First we had to sleep on the
floor, each person having
one and a half meters of
floor space. Later three-tier
beds were constructed.

In her memoirs, Ruth Klüger described Theresienstadt as a "chain of memories of missing human beings. . . a place so overcrowded, that it was virtually impossible occasionally to find a corner where you could talk to someone else. . . . I was accepted in L414, in the youngest or second youngest girls' group. L414 is one of many addresses that I will never forget. I was lucky to be accepted at all, since there was not enough room for everyone, despite assurances to the contrary. At the beginning, I saw things somewhat differently. We were thirty girls of the same age in one room, where two or three might have been comfortable. It was not a dormitory, but was the only living space. It also served as a washroom. . . . We slept in bunk beds, on straw sacks, singly or two people together. . . ."[25] Ruth Klüger also spoke of the omnipresent hunger and sporadic lessons and the physical separation of quarters and personal estrangement between Czech and German children, since the latter spoke the language of the oppressor.

The vast majority of the 4,000 works of surviving children's art from Theresienstadt was completed by Czech children during 1943 and 1944; only scattered works remain for the periods before and after these dates. There are slightly more works by girls than boys. Many of the drawings carry the students' names, barracks number, and date of work.

Marianne Lang
Pencil on paper
Born February 27, 1932
Deported to Terezín
July 2, 1942
Deported to Auschwitz
October 6, 1944
Perished
The Jewish Museum, Prague
#135.009v

34

Milan (Marvan) Eisler
Pencil on paper
Born July 29, 1932
Deported to Terezín
June 13, 1942
Survived
The Jewish Museum, Prague
#135.086

Three of the artistically most precocious Czech Theresienstadt teenagers, Jehuda Bacon (born 1929), Helga Weissová-Hosková (born 1929), and Frederick Terna (born 1924) became professional artists after the war.[26] Bacon was housed in L417, where he participated in *Vedem* and studied art there with professional artists, including Leo Haas, Otto Ungar, and Karel Fleischmann; whereas Weissová-Hosková was too old to study with Dicker-Brandeis and therefore drew "from the middle of a three-tier bunk bed at the window" in girls' home L410 and during walks through the ghetto. Terna studied with František Zelenka, Fritz Taussig (Fritta), and Leo Haas.

There is little evidence to show any interaction between the children of various nationalities who coexisted in adjacent rooms in the same residences. These children were usually organized by language group and age in separate rooms, each containing about thirty children. They were separated by nationality and language as well as by their age and experiences before deportation to Theresienstadt. Thus Dutch children had sometimes already experienced incarceration at Westerbork before arrival at Theresienstadt and had thus developed some survival skills, whereas for Czech children, Theresienstadt was their first deportation experience.

Moreover, Protestant or Catholic children of mixed marriages were often bewildered by the changed milieu from intact nuclear families to collective children's residences. It is not fully clear whether the separation of children's homes on gender lines is reflected in their art work. Thus, we know the most about Czech children and their art at Theresienstadt and very little about the others, since few works by German, Austrian, or Dutch children survived.

In addition to drawings and paintings, there were also musical and theater performances, that attempted to transmit national, ethnic, and religious traditions to the young. The Czech children's theater repertoire included Hans Krása's opera for children *Brundibár* and Karafiat's classic fairy tale *Glow Worm*, performed with a children's chorus. Children also performed in concerts, puppet performances, and other plays.

Similarly, for the children of Theresienstadt, play and sport were forms of education, exercise, and sometimes defiance. Play became a mechanism for children to cope with their surroundings, a way to channel fear and rage constructively.[27] Thus, when children in Theresienstadt played war, the Jews and Russians always won, never the Germans.

Hana Karplus
Watercolor
Born January 4, 1930
Deported to Terezín
June 4, 1942
Deported to Auschwitz
October 6, 1944
Perished
The Jewish Museum, Prague
#121.665

36

Toys were among the many items which Jews were not allowed to bring into Theresienstadt. Materials to build toys and games for children had to be scavenged and improvised. Frequently, dolls and animal figures were made of cotton wool and snippets of cloth for younger children. One painted wooden butterfly toy on wheels was made by an unknown artisan in the ghetto carpentry workshop. Since children confined in ghettos were usually not permitted to bring pets or their own toys and games, they improvised in creating these objects, thereby linking their temporary respite in children's homes with the remembered normal world of the past that had been lost. Butterflies were frequently used in the children's own drawings and poetry symbolizing freedom and flight above the ghetto reality.[28] More elaborate games were also adapted from memory with adult help.

A Theresienstadt monopoly game for children was designed by the engineer Oswald Pöck in 1943, for "buying, renting, and selling property." It was based on the original

Butterfly toy on wheels made of painted wood and wire by an anonymous artisan in the ghetto carpentry workshop in Theresienstadt according to a drawing by Professor Miloš Bic, a Protestant clergyman imprisoned in the Small Fortress.

Terezín Memorial
Copy courtesy United States
Holocaust Memorial Museum
Photo Archives
w/s #N00049

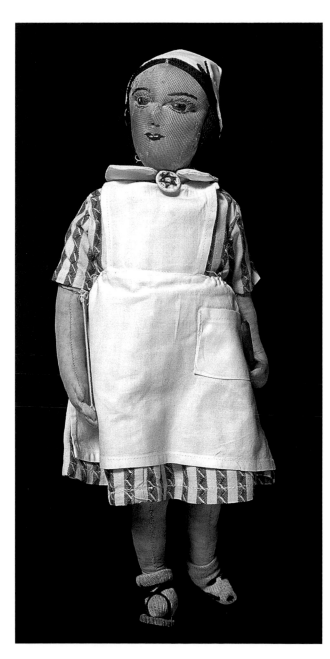

American game of 1935 that was already well-known in Europe.[29] In Theresienstadt, the game involved buying or renting locally desirable property, such as, "kumbals" or private residences built in attics, the café, the bath, etc.[30] Children thus coped with traumatic realities by incorporating them into their games, exemplified by this monopoly set.

The surviving children's art of Theresienstadt form a tragic continuum to the work of adult artists. Thus the Czech artist Bedřich Fritta made an illustrated children's book with the subject of "What will you be when you grow up?" for the third birthday of his son Tommy in January 1944. The work, still reprinted today, has become a posthumous classic.[31] Although Fritta was subsequently killed in Auschwitz-Birkenau, Tommy Fritta survived with the assistance of the artist Leo Haas, who adopted him after the war.[32]

Handmade dolls

Two dolls made by Erna Bonn, Czech, born July 7, 1896, deported to Terezín April 18, 1942; and liberated on a special transport to Switzerland on February 5, 1945.

On the left, a nurse wearing a Star of David pin, her right shoe missing; and a doll of the child deportee carrying two bags marked "Susi Vessela, Au-We 6." The latter is probably a transport number. The two dolls were donated to Beit Terezin by Selda Ehlers, Denmark.

Beit Theresienstadt, Givat Haim-Ihud, Israel   Photographs by Jeffrey Hurwitz

38

Walter Weiss
Pen and ink on tracing paper
Jewelry designs
Collection of Ela Weissberger

Rings, brooches, necklaces,
and other jewelry were produced
from various materials at
Theresienstadt and were
especially popular among younger
inmates. Such decorative objects
were sometimes inscribed with
names and transport numbers.
The jewelry was used for gifts
among friends as well as for sale.

Jewelry from Theresienstadt
H. G. Adler, *Theresienstadt 1941–1945:
Das Antlitz einer Zwangsgemeinschaft*, 2d exp.
ed. (Tübingen, 1960)
Courtesy Professor Jeremy Adler, London

THE HERITAGE OF THERESIENSTADT

Theresienstadt, like other ghettos and internment camps both in the east and west, had a wide variety of cultural, educational, and sports programs, usually developed by the prisoners. The works of professional artists were supplemented by the work of talented amateurs.[33] Ghetto workshops produced art and decorative objects for German personnel and employed artists such as Hilda Zadikowá, Charlotta Burešová, and the sculptor Richard Saudek. The artists and teachers worked mostly between 1942 and 1944, although the ghetto population constantly changed with ongoing deportations and deaths.

The mythology of this art and cultural life has served to obscure the significance and place of Theresienstadt in the process of genocide. This myth was reinforced during Communist rule, emphasizing the fate of the political resistance in the sanitized setting of the Small Fortress. Alfred Kantor, in his well-known Diary, explained that he used art as a mnemonic device to imprint events in Theresienstadt, Schwarzheide, and Auschwitz in his memory. After the war, he wrote: "... my commitment to drawing came out of a deep instinct for self-preservation and undoubtedly helped me to deny the unimaginable horrors of life at that time. By taking the role of observer, I could at least for a few moments detach myself from what was going on...and was therefore better able to hold together the threads of my sanity."[34]

Viktor Ullmann stated in the summer of 1944 in Terezín: "By no means did we sit weeping by the rivers of Babylon...our endeavors in the arts were commensurate with our will to live." This complex artistic heritage of Theresienstadt requires further analysis by the postwar world, since the tolerated and clandestine art obscures the true purpose of Theresienstadt: a means to kill tens of thousands as well as a reflection of the indomitable will of the prisoners to document their surroundings and conditions.

The surviving art of Theresienstadt also fills an important gap in twentieth century art history, providing alternatives to official war art and the bombastic stereotypes of Nazi propaganda art. Moreover, it shows us the fragility of culture and human life in a site of inhumanity. This art also functions as a bond and common language, and creates a form of visual communication and understanding about the setting for us today.

Josef Spier
Train to Auschwitz
Watercolor and ink, n.d.
Leo Baeck Institute, New York

NOTES

1. Before 1918, the town was known by the German name Theresienstadt; when Czechoslovakia became an independent nation after World War I, the name was changed to Terezín. The town was again renamed Theresienstadt under German occupation after 1938. In this essay, "Terezín" is used for the geographic place name today, and "Theresienstadt" for the ghetto during the period 1941 to 1945.

2. After June 1940, the Small Fortress was under the jurisdiction of the Prague Gestapo. From 1940 to 1945, the Small Fortress held more than 32,000 political prisoners.

3. Such deception was not uncommon. During 1940 the murder of handicapped Jews inside the Reich had been hidden by an elaborate masquerade known as the Chelm or Cholm destination. This deception even misled the Nuremberg prosecutors, and was only uncovered by the postwar German judiciary. See Henry Friedlander, *The Origins of Nazi Genocide: From Euthanasia to the Final Solution* (Chapel Hill, NC, 1995), 263–83. See also Margalit Shlain, "Ein neues Dokument zu den betrügerischen Methoden der Nazis," in *Theresienstadt in der "Endlösung der Judenfrage,"* ed. Miroslav Karny, Vojtěch Blodig, and Margita Karna (Prague, 1992), 223–32.

4. The Law for the Confiscation of Subversive and Enemy Property of July 14, 1933, was initially used for the seizure of assets (property and possessions) of proscribed and denaturalized political opponents, thereby impoverishing them. This law was also applied inside Nazi Germany to Jews (until the Eleventh decree to the Reich Citizenship Law of November 25, 1941), which provided for automatic loss of citizenship and confiscation of property if a German Jew took up residence outside the borders of the German Reich; involuntary deportation to the eastern territories occupied by the Wehrmacht counted as such a change of residence. The provisions of this law were extended to Roma and Sinti ("Gypsies") in the Twelfth decree of the Reich Citizenship Law on April 25, 1943.

5. Henry Friedlander, "The Deportation of the German Jews: Postwar German Trials of Nazi Criminals," *Leo Baeck Institute Yearbook* 29 (1984), 210–18; and H. G. Adler, *Der verwaltete Mensch: Studien zur Deportation der Juden aus Deutschland* (Tübingen, 1974), 403ff.

6. Eberhard Kolb, *Bergen-Belsen: Vom "Aufenthaltslager" zum Konzentrationslager 1943–1945* (Göttingen, 1985), 19–30; and Miroslav Karny, "Zur Typologie des Theresienstädter Konzentrationslagers," *Judaica Bohemiae* 17, no.1 (1981): 3–14.

7. See Miroslav Karny, "Theresienstadt und Auschwitz," *1999: Zeitschrift für Sozialgeschichte des 20. und 21. Jahrhunderts* 3, no. 3 (1988): 9–26; and idem, "The Genocide of the Czech Jews," in *Terezín Memorial Book: Jewish Victims of Nazi Deportations from Bohemia and Moravia* (Prague, 1996), 27–87, 110–11.

8. Bronka Klibanski, "Kinder aus dem Ghetto Bialystok in Theresienstadt," *Theresienstädter Studien und Dokumente* (1995), 92–105.

9. Vojtěch Blodig, "Die letzte Phase der Entwicklung des Ghettos Theresienstadt," in *Theresienstadt in der "Endlösung der Judenfrage,"* 267–78; Lenore Lappin, "Der Weg ungarischer Juden nach Theresienstadt," *Theresienstädter Studien und Dokumente* (1996), 52–81; and Katarina Hradska, "Vorgeschichte der slowakischen Transporte nach Theresienstadt," ibid., 82–97.

10. Joseph Kermish, ed., *To Live with Honor and Die with Honor!...: Selected Documents from the Warsaw Ghetto Underground Archives "O.S." ["Oneg Shabbath"]* (Jerusalem, 1986). For the secret archives of the Kovno ghetto, see United States Holocaust Memorial Museum, ed., *Hidden History of the Kovno Ghetto* (Boston, New York, Toronto, and London, 1997), 149f.

11. Janet Blatter and Sybil Milton, *Art of the Holocaust* (New York, 1981); and Sybil Milton, "Kunst als historisches Quellenmaterial in Gedenkstätten und Museen," in *über-lebens-mittel: Kunst aus Konzentrationslager und in Gedenkstätten für die Opfer des Nationalsozialismus,* ed. Wulff E. Brebeck, Angela Genger, Thomas Lutz, and others (Marburg, 1992), 44–63.

12. H. G. Adler, *Theresienstadt 1941–1945: Das Antlitz einer Zwangsgemeinschaft,* 2d exp. ed. (Tübingen, 1960), note 349b on 850–51. The Lautsch company owned by Oskar Perschke, a non-Jew, was located in Prague in 1939, and served as a place of employment for his wife's Jewish relatives. When his in-laws had been deported to Theresienstadt in February 1942, Perschke negotiated with the Economic Department of the SS commandant's office to set up workshops at Theresienstadt to produce artistic and decorative objects for SS personnel at Theresienstadt and for export to German companies. The

Theresienstadt workshops were closed in September 1943. See Arno Pařík, "Art in the Terezín Ghetto," *Seeing through "Paradise": Artists and the Terezín Concentration Camp* (Boston, 1991), 54.

13. Karel Margry, "'Theresienstadt' (1944–1945): The Nazi Propaganda Film Depicting the Concentration Camp as Paradise," *Historical Journal of Film, Radio, and Television* 12, no.2 (1992): 149–51. The Dutch artist Jo Spier made hundreds of sketches as the film was shot, creating a visual log book enabling Karel Margry to reconstruct the entire film since 1987. The surviving fragments of the film included children playing, a soccer match in the courtyard of the Dresden barracks, the nursery school, health care for children, and the staging of the children's opera *Brundibár*. See Margry, 155–58.

14. Thirteen artists (ten Czech, two Austrian, and one Dutch) were associated with Technical Department: the Czechs included Adolf Aussenberg, Albin Glaser, Leo Haas, Leo Heilbrunn, Petr Kien, František Lustig, Fritz Taussig (known as Fritta), Norbert Troller, Otto Ungar, Ludvik Wodak; the Austrians Ferdinand Bloch, Oswald Pöck; and the Dutch Josef Spier. At least seven artists were connected with the Lautsch company workshops, including Elsbeth Argustinska, Charlotta Burešová, Otto Karas, František Moric Nagl, Hilda Zadikowá, Richard Saudek, and Arnold Zadikow. Fourteen additional artists at Theresienstadt included three Czech physicians Pavel Fantl, Moritz Müller, and Karel Fleischmann; the artist-educator Friedl Dicker-Brandeis; the prolific caricaturist Max Placek; Alfred Bergel, Felix Bloch, Alfred Kantor, Otto Karas-Kaufman, Malvina Schalkova, Julie Wolfthorn, František Zelenka, and two anonymous artists known by their initials J. L. and E. K. In addition to these thirty-four artists, other artists had been assigned to provide sketches and stage sets for theater and film productions in the ghetto.

15. Gerald Green, *The Artists of Terezín* (New York, 1978); Leo Haas, "The affair of the painters of Terezín," in *Seeing through "Paradise,"* 63–68.

16. Ludmila Chládková, "Die Theresienstädter Kindereine Bilanz," in *Theresienstadt in der "Endlösung der Judenfrage,"* 173–78. Chládková challenges the dramatic myth of one hundred surviving children based on an analysis of the transports into Theresienstadt from December 1941 to May 1945. The 1,569 surviving children under the age of fifteen and

Norbert Troller
Man with Cup
Watercolor
Theresienstadt, 1942
Estate of the artist, Doris Rausch;
Troller Collection, Leo Baeck Institute

Josef Bauml
Watercolor
Born March 13, 1931
Deported to Terezín
July 7, 1942
Deported to Auschwitz
October 12, 1944
Perished
The Jewish Museum, Prague
#131.778

an additional 174 children who had reached the age of fifteen in the ghetto included: 512 children from the Protectorate (including part Jews who had arrived in the ghetto after January 1945); 243 from the German Reich and its incorporated territories (including Lodz in the Wartheland); seventy-two from Austria; 265 from the Netherlands; forty-three from Denmark; 312 from Slovakia; and 293 from Hungary. Moreover sixty-six children under fifteen years old were included in the transport of 1,200 Jews released from Theresienstadt to Switzerland on February 5, 1945. An additional forty-one children had been born and survived in Theresienstadt. Adler, *Theresienstadt 1941–1945*, 572–73 estimates that about 9,000 children had been incarcerated in Theresienstadt, ca. six and one-half percent of the ghetto population, and that ca. 1,644 children were alive in May 1945. Cháldková defines children as under fifteen years old, H. G. Adler's statistics uses seventeen as the cut-off age.

17. Adler, *Theresienstadt, 1941–1945*, 562–73.

18. Ruth Klüger, *Weiter leben: Eine Jugend* (Göttingen, 1992), 80–104.

19. Sybil Milton, ed. and trans., *Innocence and Persecution: The Art of Jewish Children in Nazi Germany, 1936–1941* (New York, 1989); Nicholas Stargardt, "Children's Art of the Holocaust," *Past and Present* (Nov. 1998), 191–235; and Berufsverband Bildender Künstler Schwaben-Nord und Augsburg e.V., ed., *Kinderzeichnungen aus dem Konzentrationslager Theresienstadt* (Augsburg, 1990).

20. Elena Makarova, *From Bauhaus to Terezín: Friedl Dicker-Brandeis and Her Pupils* (Jerusalem, 1990); Anita Frankova, "Theresienstädter Erziehung," and "Berichte zum ersten Jahrestag der Theresienstädter Heime in L 417," *Theresienstädter Studien und Dokumente* (1998), 142–80; see especially texts by Berta Freund "Erziehung ist Kunst, Kunst ist Erziehung" at pp. 164–65 and Friederike (Friedl) Dicker-Brandeis, "Kinderzeichen" at pp. 175–78.

21. Fredy Hirsch, unpublished text, from the Jewish Museum in Prague, copy courtesy of Hannelore Wonschick, Berlin.

22. Elena Makarova, *Friedl Dicker-Brandeis: Ein Leben für Kunst und Lehre* (Vienna and Munich, 1999), 34.

23. Marie Rút Krizková, Kurt Kiri Kotouc, and Zdenek Ornest, ed., *We are Children Just the Same: Vedem, the Secret Magazine by the*

Boys of Terezín, transl. R. Elizabeth Novak (Philadelphia, 1995),
35. See also Erik Pollak, "Die Bedeutung der Zeitschriften im Leben der Theresienstädter Kinder und Jugend," in *Theresienstadt in der "Endlösung der Judenfrage,"* 165; and Jarmila Skochova, "Détekij dom I v L417 (Respublika Skid) v konclagere Terezín," *Judaica Bohemia*, 3 parts in no. 1 (1978): 3–14, no.2 (1980): 91–102, and no.1 (1981): 47 ff.

24. Ibid.

25. Klüger, 85–87.

26. Helga Weissová, *Zeichne, was Du siehst: Zeichnungen eines Kindes aus Theresienstadt/Terezín* (Göttingen, 1998); H. G. Adler, "Yehuda Bacon," in *Mit der Ziehharmonika: Zeitschrift für Literatur des Exils und des Widerstands* 10, no.2 (July 1993): 4–6; Yehuda Bacon, "Mein Leben im 'Jugendheim,'" reprinted from H. G. Adler, *Theresienstadt*, 552–57 and 709–11. For Terna, *Seeing through "Paradise,"* 32.

27. See George Eisen, *Children and Play in the Holocaust: Games among the Shadows* (Amherst, 1988).

28. Hana Volavková, ed., *. . . I never saw another butterfly . . . : Children's Drawings and Poems from Terezín Concentration Camp, 1942–1944*, 2d rev. exp. ed. by the United States Holocaust Memorial Museum (New York, 1993).

29. See www.monopoly.com for the history and rules of "Monopoly."

30. There are reports that monopoly was also played in 1943 at Westerbork transit camp in the occupied Netherlands. See Philip Mechanicus, *Year of Fear: A Jewish Prisoner Waits for Auschwitz* (New York, 1968), 129, 159.

31. Bedřich Fritta, *Tomickovi* (The Hague, 1980), also published in German and English editions.

32. Dorothea Stanic, *Kinder im KZ* (Berlin, 1979), 128–30.

33. See Norbert Troller, *Theresienstadt: Hitler's Gift to the Jews*, trans. Susan E. Cernyak-Spatz (Chapel Hill, NC, 1991); Wolf H. Wagner, *Der Hölle entronnen: Stationen eines Lebens; Eine Biographie des Malers und Graphikers Leo Haas* (Berlin, 1987), 66–112; *Seeing through "Paradise."*

34. Alfred Kantor, *The Book of Alfred Kantor* (New York, 1971), unpaginated.

Bedřich Hoffmann
Pencil
Born April 4, 1932
Deported to Terezín
September 30, 1942
Deported to Aushwitz
October 19, 1944
The Jewish Museum, Prague
#133.065

44

Theresienstadt was marked after 1941 by an atmosphere of permanent insecurity and lack of privacy. The first deportees to Theresienstadt in 1941 found a small and dilapidated town with unsanitary conditions: fleas, lice, accumulated refuse, and contaminated wells. The small courtyards of Theresienstadt had previously been used as chicken coops, pigsties, and even as vegetable gardens. It took several months to clean this up.

The ghetto was ostensibly managed by a Jewish administration known as the Council of Elders (*the Ältestenrat*), although this "self-government" was stringently controlled by the Germans.

Some fragments of civilian life before deportation remained in Theresienstadt, contributing to the veneer of normality. For example, the appearance of a normal town was maintained through the ghetto's internal administration which included departments for housing, health, finance, culture, a youth welfare office, and an economic department to distribute food and assign work in the ghetto.

Initially, there were no hospital facilities or medical equipment. By 1942, some supplies had been accumulated from medicines brought by individual deportees and medical supplies sent by Jewish hospitals and sanitoria in Germany and Bohemia.

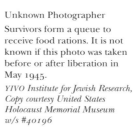

Norbert Troller
Transport
Pencil on paper
Theresienstadt, 1942
Estate of the artist, Doris Rauch;
Troller Collection, Leo Baeck Institute,
New York

Unknown Photographer
Survivors form a queue to receive food rations. It is not known if this photo was taken before or after liberation in May 1945.
YIVO Institute for Jewish Research,
Copy courtesy United States
Holocaust Memorial Museum
w/s #40196

Unknown Photographer
Typhus ward in Theresienstadt
barracks, probably after
liberation, 1945
*YIVO Institute for Jewish Research,
Copy courtesy United States Holocaust
Memorial Museum*
w/s #40228

45

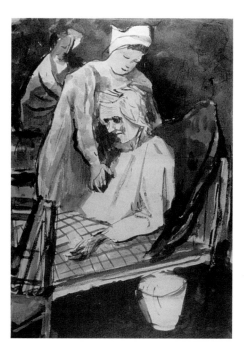

Otto Ungar
Hospital Ward in Theresienstadt
Watercolor on paper, n.d.
Collection of Joža Karas

The existing hospital building was inadequate for the enormous number of ill patients, and auxiliary sick bays were set up in many of the barracks.

The prisoners included many prominent physicians and medical specialists, but laypeople often carried out most of the nursing care. Most of the prisoners who died in Theresienstadt succumbed to exhaustion, malnutrition, and epidemics.

The dead were buried in individual graves until August 1942; thereafter, mass graves were dug to accommodate up to thirty-six coffins. The Germans would not allow Jews to bury their dead in fabric shrouds, and thus corpses were often wrapped in paper to fulfill religious requirements for internment. In October 1942, a crematorium—forbidden by Jewish tradition—was set up, and the Germans forced Jewish prisoners to operate the ovens. The ashes of individuals were stored and marked for identification, but in November 1944, these urns were emptied into the Ohre River.

Helga Weissová-Hosková
The Last Farewell
Pen and ink, 1944
*Wallstein Verlag,
Göttingen, Germany*

. . . This evening I walked alond the street of death.
    On one wagon, they were taking the dead away.

Why so many marches have been drummed here?

Why so many soldiers?

Then
    A week after the end,
    Everything will be empty here.
    A hungry dove will peck for bread.
    In the middle of the street will stand
    An empty, dirty
    Hearse.

Anonymous
extract from "The Closed Town," in Hana Valavková, ed.,
*. . . I never saw another butterfly. . . Children's Drawings and Poems
from Terezín Concentration Camp 1942–44*, (New York, 1993), 5

Ivan Vojtěch Fric
Close-up of a man wearing a
yellow star on ghetto street.
Behind him a man pulls a
wagon with bread rations,
February 1944
*United States Holocaust
Memorial Museum w/s #20260*

Helga Weissová-Hosková
Bread on the Hearses
Watercolor on paper
December 27, 1942

The universal means of transportation in the ghetto were hearses from disbanded Jewish communitities, without their elaborate super-structures. These were used to haul luggage of new arrivals, bread, and elderly persons.

Jugendfürsorge (Welfare for the Young) is written on this hearse. Note that a child is using the wagon as a game (the girl on the back having hitched a ride).

*Wallstein Verlag,
Göttingen, Germany*

48

Ghetto currency
Collection of Ela Weissberger

The finance department set wage rates in ghetto currency issued by the Council of Elders after January 1943; in reality, this currency was worthless scrip. The scrip had been printed by the National Bank of Prague, and the State Printing Works created paper money used exclusively by Jews in the Theresienstadt ghetto. In late April 1943, a so-called Bank of the Jewish Self-Government, located in the former town hall of Theresienstadt, received fifty-three million Theresienstadt Kronen (crowns).

Since there was nothing to buy, the new ghetto monetary system necessitated the creation of a simulated system of bookkeeping, whereby inmates kept worthless passbooks and accounts reflecting supposed payrolls and imaginary salaries or savings.

The only place where money was actually used or "spent" was the ghetto library, where the loan of each book required a 50 Kronen deposit.

By 1944, the bank account of the Theresienstadt library contained 120,000 Kronen on deposit. Nevertheless, ghetto scrip was

used during the Red Cross inspection to foster the illusion that prisoners received salaries for their labor and that goods were available for purchase. One scene in the 1944 film *Theresienstadt: A Documentary Film from the Jewish Settlement* shows long lines of elderly Jews with ghetto scrip, their savings passbooks in hand, standing in front of the "bank" to deposit their savings. These deliberate and elaborate deceptions permeated every aspect of daily life in the ghetto.

The intricate mirage of the ghetto included the official ghetto economy, including money, culture, and "beautification," all central aspects of German control.

Savings passbook issued by the Bank of the Jewish Self-Government in Theresienstadt for Stefanie(?) Bassist, transport number Ar 371, housed in L308.

The left side shows several pages marked "*Gesperrtes Guthaben*," or blocked account with 675 kronen.

Only the deposit column is filled in, since no one could withdraw money from their account.

Simon Wiesenthal Museum of Tolerance, Los Angeles

Labor identity card from Theresienstadt ghetto for Walter Weiss, born March 31, 1912, issued on October 25, 1943

Assignment: mechanic.

The left side of the card stipulates:

1) Every ghetto inhabitant is required to carry this labor card with them at all times and to show it as required to the authorities.

2) He is required to provide his labor identity card during transfers, change of labor

assignments, for out-patient treatment if ill, to receive medications from the pharmacy, and if reclassified by work registration office.

3) He is required to have his work free day registered in his labor identity card by the appropriate labor office.

4) Violations of these regulations will be punished. Similarly, any unauthorized changes in the particulars of this labor card will be punished.

Collection of Ela Weissberger

Nevertheless, ghetto currency—often cigarettes rather than official scrip—could purchase extra food, access to the laundry or bathhouse, and medicines.

The only commodity that could not be sold was exemption from deportation.

Packages and food parcels sent by relatives and friends were allowed in the ghetto, and occasionally even reached the intended recipient.

Postcard receipts for these packages informed those outside the ghetto whether the recipient was alive, and occasionally small clandestine messages could be conveyed on such postal forms.

Prague 25 April 1944

Dear Friedl,
Above all, best wishes from everyone as well as from Lange and Trude. Have you received our greetings from the first of the month? Why do neither Paul nor you write? We are worried about you. Everything is unchanged for us, which is the main reason for my apology that I write so infrequently. Next week, we again want to write to Dr. Fritai, so that each of you will alternately receive news from us, first one of you, then the other. Best wishes and greetings to you, Paul, and all friends, I remain your brother-in-law, Otto.

Translation by Sybil H. Milton

Postcard to Friedl Dicker-Brandeis from her brother-in-law, Otto Brandeis

Note the date stamp on the front of the card which is almost one month later, May 24, 1944, indicating the delays in censored mail to prisoners. The postcard hints at the nondelivery of mail to Theresienstadt prisoners.

Simon Wiesenthal Museum of Tolerance, Los Angeles

Helga Weissová-Hosková
Getting a Parcel
Ink on paper
January 13, 1944
Wallstein Verlag, Göttingen, Germany

50

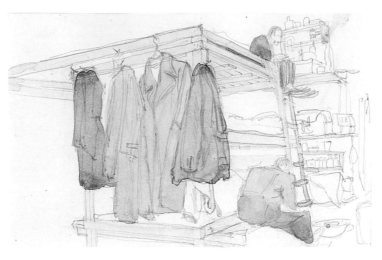

Norbert Troller
Men's Quarters
Watercolor on paper, n.d.
Estate of the artist, Doris Rauch;
Troller Collection, Leo Baeck Institute,
New York

Friedl Dicker-Brandeis
People in Bunk Beds
Charcoal on paper, n.d.
Simon Wiesenthal Museum
of Tolerance, Los Angeles

AN INSECURE PRESENT; AN UNCERTAIN FUTURE

Housing was segregated by gender, with separate facilities for the disabled and infants. Women were housed in the Hamburg and Dresden barracks, each holding 3,000 inmates. Individual rooms held up to thirty individuals. Men were assigned quarters in the Sudeten barracks, holding up to 5,000 men sleeping on the floor or in three-story bunk beds. After work during the day, families were allowed to meet for two hours in the women's barracks.

There were few places for couples to conduct courtships or make love; the coal bunker was the most popular location for brief moments of tenderness. Most of the children in Theresienstadt were forced to live in separate barracks apart from their parents; there too conditions were overcrowded, unsanitary, and disease-ridden.

There was no freedom, not enough food, and fear was omnipresent. Hunger and insecurity were constant features of daily life.

Norbert Troller
My Nightmare
Watercolor on paper
Theresienstadt, 1943

Troller uses the ladder-like shelves of an endless bunk bed topped by the arriving angel of death. There are also allegorical references to Jacob's ladder, stacked bakery trays, and overcrowded bunk bed quarters. Troller spent a lot of time sketching the ghetto bakery in Theresienstadt, where his works were hidden and later retrieved.

Estate of the artist, Doris Rauch; Troller Collection, Leo Baeck Institute, New York

ART AS COMMODITY, RESISTANCE, AND FOR SURVIVAL

The Jews in Theresienstadt worked valiantly, often in secret and at peril, to create a vibrant and diversified cultural life. The noted Berlin Rabbi Leo Baeck, who had refused an offer to be rescued, was one of dozens of scholars and teachers who lectured regularly to audiences who stood due to lack of chairs. Alongside a daily schedule of lectures on topics ranging from science to philosophy, literature to Zionism, a library of about 50,000 volumes was amassed and in constant use. There were also regular theatrical and musical performances of classics like Verdi's *Requiem* as well as original choral, orchestral, and jazz compositions.

The rich cultural life at Theresienstadt also contained ambiguities. The SS allowed a kind of freedom of speech and did not censor either lectures or theater productions. Obviously, the Germans believed that such control was immaterial, since the prisoners would all ultimately be killed.

Nevertheless, for the prisoners, the chimera of even a temporary normality, enabled them to create a temporary sense of community and the tools of survival. Art was a commodity, sold for food and survival, and also a form of resistance and a strategy for survival.

Monopoly Game
Beit Theresienstadt, Givat Haim-Ihud, Israel

52

"SMELINA"—BLACK MARKET MONOPOLY GAME

The monopoly game was made in the Theresienstadt ghetto by the engineer Oswald Pöck (b. October 2, 1893; deported from Prague to Terezín on November 30, 1941; deported from Terezín to Auschwitz-Birkenau on September 29, 1944, perished).

Smelina in Czech colloquial usage of the war years and immediate postwar period meant "deception" or "swindle" and refers to deceptive black market businesses hidden from the SS in Theresienstadt. *Smelina* also meant "black-marketeer."

On the monopoly game board, properties were named after camp landmarks and buildings. After buying a set of properties, an investor could increase the value of a building by building a *kumbal* (attic residence) instead of houses or hotels. Camp scrip in "ghetto kronen" were used in the game. The center of the board shows rows of barracks in the ghetto. The game is based on the original Parker Brothers board game invented in the United States and well distributed throughout Europe in the 1930s.

The monopoly game was always left behind when children were transported from Theresienstadt to camps in the East and was last owned by Micha and Dan Glass at Theresienstadt; they subsequently donated it to Beit Theresienstadt, Givat Haim-Ihud, Israel.

A "Bank Selbstver[waltung]"– Bank of the Jewish Self-Government

B Chance

1 Start

2 "Hohenelber"– Hohenelbe barracks

The Hohenelbe barracks contained the central ghetto hospital.

3 "Kavalier"– Cavalier barracks

This barracks housed elderly and mentally ill prisoners and had served as a *schleuse* ("conduit" or "funnel") where arriving Jewish deportees were registered and their possessions robbed in 1942.

4 "Produktion"– Production

5 "Entwesung"– Disinfection (delousing station)

6 "Spedition"–Shipping or Moving

7 Chance

8 "Bauhof"– Lumberyard workshops

The Bauhof contained workshops where inmates constructed their own beds and simple furniture as well as filled special orders for the German ghetto administration.

9 "Post"– Post Office

10 "Aussiger"– Aussig barracks

This barracks contained the central clothing warehouse as well as the first *schleuse* or conduit.

11 "Gefängnis"– Prison

12 "Kaffeehaus"– Café

13 "Elektriz[ität]"– Electricity (Power)

14 "Freizeitgest[altung]"– "Recreational" activities

15 "Bastei"– Bastion

16 "Küche"– Kitchen

17 "Zeughaus"– Arsenal

18 Chance

19 "Bodenbacher"– Bodenbach barracks

This barracks contained prisoner dormitories and the *schleuse*. In July 1943, they were evacuated and then used as an archive for the RSHA [Reichssicherheitshauptamt or Central Office for Reich Security] that had been relocated from Berlin to Theresienstadt.

20 "Dresdner"– Dresden barracks

The Dresden barracks housed women and at first, also their children. Later separate children's homes were opened. There was a prison in the cellar. Soccer was permitted in the barracks yard.

21 "Dekade"– "Taking a Break"

The ghetto Labor Department divided each month into three *decades* or terms. Each work assignment was linked to the receipt of a ration coupon, which was also referred to as a *Dekade* by ghetto inmates. If the agricultural fields required workers, ghetto inmates said that one was ordered *auf Dekade*, or "to go on a decade," which meant going on holiday or taking a break, something not legally possible in the ghetto. In the ghettos and camps, new code words such as *Dekade* emerged to describe specific local conditions.

22 "Genie"– Genie barracks

The Genie barracks contained the hospital and dormitories for the elderly.

23 "Bank d[er] jüd[ischen] Selbstver[waltung]"–Bank of the Jewish Self-Government

24 "Hamburger"– Hamburg barracks

This barracks contained women's dormitories and after 1943 held mostly Dutch prisoners. It was also used a *schleuse* for transports to Auschwitz.

25 "G.W. Kas" [Ghetto Wache Kaserne]– Ghetto guards barracks

26 "Fleischer"– Butcher

27 "Jugendheim"– Children's home

28 "Wasserwerk"– Water tower

29 "Zentralbad"– Central baths

30 "Reitschule"– Riding school

The former military riding school was converted into a joiner's workshop in the ghetto.

31 "Geh ins Gefängnis"–"Go to Jail"

The drawings shows a ghetto policeman ordering an inmate to report to jail.

32 "Bäckerei"– Bakery (also the main food warehouse)

33 "Landwirtsch[aft]"– Agriculture (farming and gardening)

34 Chance

35 "Jägerkas[erne]"– Jäger Barracks

This barracks served as dormitories for elderly male prisoners and also as a quarantine station.

36 "Proviantur"– Food and supplies warehouse

37 "Bank d[er] jüd[ischen] Selbstver[waltung]"–Bank of the Jewish Self-Government

38 "Hannover"– Hanover barracks

This barracks contained one of the ghetto kitchens and also dormitories for working men.

39 "Schleuse"–The Sluice or funnel

A conduit where arriving transports were registered and personal possessions confiscated. The *schleuse* was also an assembly center for arriving or departing inmates. After a few hours or days, the prisoners were then allocated quarters or deportation transports. The *schleuse* was situated in various barracks and buildings and had no central site.

40 "Magdeburg"– Magdeburg barracks

This barracks contained the offices of the Council of Elders and the administration of the Jewish self-government. It included offices as well as apartments for members of the self-government and a hall for cultural events.

54

11 "Gefängnis"– Prison

RULES FOR PLAYING "SMELINA"

Smelina is a dice game involving the purchase and selling of real estate and similar properties. The basic rules of play are:

Up to five individuals can play this game. The players throw the dice and the player with the highest number begins first. Each player has a different color figure, which is moved across the board squares according to the value of the dice number. Every player can buy the square on which he/she stands, until all properties have been purchased. In owning a property, the player, e.g. Central bath, possibly costing 300 kronen, the owner is allowed to demand rent, e.g. renting the bath costs eighteen kronen.

The following rents are allowed: Entering the Magdeburg barracks costs a rent of thirty kronen; entering the transport costs five times the number on the dice; e.g. if the number six is on the dice, the person pays thirty kronen.

If all properties have been bought, the player must attempt to aquire a color series, e.g. the Bastei (bastion) and Kaffehaus (café) belong to the "recreation" activities (yellow series), the various barracks compose the red series, while the electricity works, water works, kitchen and schleuse, etc. belong to the picture series, and so forth.

An example: if player x owns the Bastei and the Kaffehaus, but he doesn't own the entire "recreation department," which is owned by player y, then player x must attempt to purchase the missing three properties from y or swap them for another property. In selling, y is allowed to charge the maximum. If a player has won an entire color series, he can purchase a kumbal. The price of a kumbal is equal to the value of the land, e.g., Magdeburg 400 kronen, in owning a kumbal the price of rent for the property depends on the price structure. If, e.g., player x has a kumbal on the Bastei (rampart or bastion), every other player can be asked to pay the kumbal rent to player x for entering the Bastei.

The game ends once all money is held either by the bank or by a player or when one of the players declares bankruptcy. If a player lands on the square for the Bank of the Jewish Self-Government or on the square marked chance, the player takes the top card from the deck indicated, follows the instructions on the card, and returns the card face down to the bottom of the deck.

For example, if a player gets 150 kronen from the bank, the game continues by the rules. If a player lands in jail, his/her turn ends. A player can get out of jail by (a) throwing doubles on the dice and then moving forward the number of spaces shown by the doubles throw; (b) drawing the "get out of jail free" card; (c) purchasing the "get out of jail" card from another player; or (d) paying a fine before rolling the dice on one of the next two turns. The players may improve and make the game more interesting by adding to the rules.

21 "Dekade"–"Taking a Break"

16 "Küche"– Kitchen

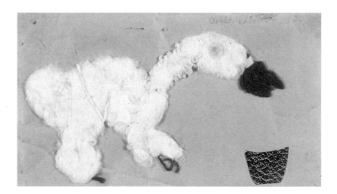

Cotton wool animal made by unknown
six to eight year old child in
Gertrude Groag's classes at Theresienstadt

Beit Theresienstadt, Givat Haim-Ihud, Israel
Photograph by Jeffrey Hurwitz

Hedvika Kantr
Pencil on paper
Born August 25, 1930
Deported to Terezín
September 4, 1942
Survived

The Jewish Museum, Prague
#131.881

56

TM #A7737

ILLUSION AND REALITY: THE RED CROSS VISITS THE "MODEL GHETTO"

On June 23, 1944, The International Red Cross Commission, made up of two Danish and one Swiss representative, Maurice Rossel, conducted a six-hour inspection of the Theresienstadt ghetto.

The visit was carefully managed and controlled by the Germans. The Red Cross officials were accompanied by a number of high-ranking SS officers, including Rolf Günther from Berlin, Ernest Möhs, who served as the liaison between Berlin and Theresienstadt, and the ghetto commandant SS First Lieutenant Karl Rahm.

The visitors were also accompanied by Eberhard von Thadden, legation councilor of the German Foreign Office, who was responsible as liaison between the Foreign Office and Eichmann's Office IVb4 in the Central Office for Reich Security.

On July 1, 1944, Maurice Rossel sent Von Thadden his report accompanied by a thank you letter. Rossel's cover note stated: "... we are pleased to repeat our assurances to you that our report about our visit to Theresienstadt will reassure many people, since conditions are satisfactory..." The report itself stated: "We must say that we are astonished to find out that the Ghetto was a community leading an almost normal existence, as we are prepared for the worst." *

Already in mid-May 1944, before the Red Cross visit, approximately 7,500 Jews had been deported from Theresienstadt to Auschwitz-Birkenau. Two-thirds of these deportees had originally been transported to Theresienstadt from Germany, Austria, and the Netherlands; one-third had come from the Protectorate of Bohemia and Moravia. This reduced the appearance of overcrowding in the ghetto. The International Red Cross Commission was permitted to inspect only the first floor rooms of barracks, and all buildings on their tour had been painted and fixed up as part of the "beautification" program in the spring of 1944. However, the upper floors of the barracks were overcrowded with the remaining inmates.

In late September 1944, after the Theresienstadt propaganda film had been completed, eleven transports with 18,402 men, women, and children were dispatched from Theresienstadt to Auschwitz-Birkenau, where most were killed.

*[This quotation is from the IRC Report, p.15, in the National Archives, Washington, DC, Record Group 84, Foreign Service Posts, American legation Bern, American Interests Section, General Records 1942–45, Box 48, 840.1 Jews-Europe, June–August 1944]

TM #A7735

TM #A799

TM #A7733

Stills from the 1944 Nazi propaganda film, *Theresienstadt: A Documentary Film from the Jewish Settlement Area*, known after the war as *The Führer Gives a Town to the Jews*. The identities of the children are unknown.

Art, Music and Education as Strategies for Survival: Theresienstadt 1941–45

On Wednesday afternoon February 14, 1945, two trains with 1,200 Jews from Theresienstadt had arrived at the Swiss border in Konstanz after a three day journey and proceeded to the town of St. Gallen. The trains included 500-600 Dutch Jews, a few Swiss nationals who had been held in Germany, and fifty-eight children under the age of twelve. St. Gallen was to be a temporary stopover for five to six days before the survivors could be sent to other Swiss refugee camps.

The Swiss photographer, Walter Scheiwiller from Zollikon, had been asked to document the arrival of these survivors in a photo story. Scheiwiller had completed his apprenticeship as a photographer at "Photohaus Zumbühl" in St. Gallen between 1939 and 1942, and subsequently became a photojournalist. He worked as a newspaper photographer in Zürich from 1942 to 1945 and as an independent photographer from 1946 to 1988. He owned a photo business in Zürich, later specializing in sports photography.

When donating these photographs to the St. Gallen City Archive in January 1996, Walter Scheiwiller recalled that he had received written instructions for a photographic story on February 11, 1945. "After a difficult three day journey, 1,200 Jewish civilians from Theresienstadt reached Switzerland as a result of the intervention of retired Swiss Federal Councilor Musy. The refugees were mostly sheltered in St. Gallen. . . . It was a sensitive and delicate assignment to document the plight of the sad refugees in photographs. . . . To photograph hundreds of emaciated and bewildered individuals in immense distress was a delicate assignment, almost insensitive and insolent of [their] human rights." His twenty-five photographs reveal the improvised quarters set up by the Red Cross for temporary housing, feeding, and medical care.

An elderly female survivor eating one of her first meals in freedom in St. Gallen, Switzerland, February 14, 1945

Photographs of temporary shelter in Hadwigschulhaus in St. Gallen, Switzerland, for some of the 1,200 Jewish survivors from Theresienstadt who had arrived in Switzerland on February 14, 1945.

Photographs by Walter Scheiwiller, February 15, 1945
Courtesy of Dr. Ernst Ziegler, Archivist St. Gallen City Archives

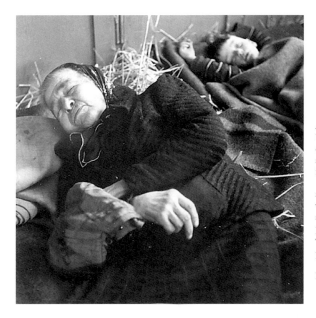

An older woman and a boy were among the exhausted survivors sleeping fully clothed on improvised bedding (straw mattresses, pillows, and blankets), together with their suitcases and sacks with their scant personal possessions.

This photograph was published in the *St. Gallen Tagblatt* on Wednesday, February 14, 1945.

One of the surviving Theresienstadt children at Hadwigschulhaus in St. Gallen, Switzerland, February 14, 1945

60

Eva Landa (Room 28)
Pencil on paper
Born December 25, 1930
Deported to Terezín
July 2, 1942
Deported to Auschwitz
December 15, 1943
Survived
The Jewish Museum, Prague
#131.814

Irka Kraus
Pencil on paper
Born April 28, 1930
Deported to Terezín
July 23, 1942
Survived
The Jewish Museum, Prague
#133.522

The children who survived deportation, internment, and death camps are the last primary witnesses of the Holocaust. Their word, and their presence, carries much authority.

In 1989, after the borders opened in Eastern and Central Europe, a group of survivors from Theresienstadt/Terezín reestablished contact with one another. All were girls between ten and twelve years old when they were deported to the Ghetto with their families during 1942 and 1943. Most were Jews from Bohemia and Moravia from upper- and middle-class backgrounds. All of them were students of Friedl Dicker-Brandeis. Artwork created by this group, referred to as "The Girls from Room 28," formed the heart of the exhibition *The Arts as Strategies for Survival: Theresienstadt 1941–45.* "The Girls" were also involved in its organization, which included generous loans of memorabilia from their years at Terezín.

The study of the Holocaust—its perpetrators, bystanders, victims; its archives and memorials; its witnesses—warn us about hate, intolerance, and the loss of human rights. The evidence of children's lives in Terezín left as drawings, paintings, and collages shows how art can express, heal, and sustain the hope of survival.

"Friedl's Girls" lived in one of the Children's Homes, L410, Room 28. Friedl Dicker-Brandeis came often to their room, and others in L410, to give art lessons. Children

HANNELORE WONSCHICK AND ANNE D. DUTLINGER
TRANSLATED BY IAN PEPPER

from other rooms sometimes participated in the lessons held in Room 28. Students came and went, arriving and departing on increasingly frequent transports.

Dicker-Brandeis studied at the Bauhaus, lived in Theresienstadt, and died in Auschwitz. Her training and teaching reflect the Weimar period and the Bauhaus, when the practice of art combined spiritual engagement, political idealism, and activism.

Although graphic design by Friedl Dicker[†] is included in every major book on the Bauhaus, it is her final work, her teaching, represented by the children's artwork from Theresienstadt, which has established her reputation. Awareness and appreciation of Dicker-Brandeis's artwork has widened due to her tragic fate , which she shared with many of her fellow modernists, and most of the other artists in Theresienstadt. How (or how much) does the Holocaust affect our reading of an artist's work, determine its value, or define its audience?

Should we "place" Friedl Dicker-Brandeis, and the art of her young students in art or history? Neither "Art of the Holocaust" nor child art is usually part of art history survey courses. If included, both tend to be treated as special categories. Art created during or from the memory of the Holocaust remains primarily the subject of historians specializing in Jewish history and culture; child art, that of art educators, psychologists, and art therapists.

Hanka Wertheimer
Watercolor
Born December 12, 1929
Deported to Terezín
March 3, 1942
Deported to Auschwitz
May 18, 1944
Survived
The Jewish Museum, Prague
#131.688

The art and memoirs of "Friedl's Girls" from Room 28 provide a unique opportunity combine perspectives—to witness life during the Holocaust, to consider the interplay between child art, modern art, and the mutual influences between teacher and student.

Dicker-Brandeis's decision to use her time in Terezín teaching art to children, remarkable in itself, gave her young students both structure and freedom. Alongside the color studies and exercises in drawing are lessons of friendship and hope. The artwork from Terezín left behind by both child and adult artists continues to stun the eye and move the heart. The voices of "Friedl's Girls" clearly remind us of the obligation of the living—to see, to listen, and to speak.

Anne D. Dutlinger
Curator, *The Arts as Strategies for Survival: Theresienstadt 1941–45*

[†] After marriage to Pavel Brandeis in 1936, Friedl Dicker took his last name.

Lenka Lindt
Pencil on paper
Born March 19, 1930
Deported to Terezín
February 15, 1942
Deported to Auschwitz
October 28, 1944
Perished
The Jewish Museum, Prague
#135.028r

The Girls from Room 28 L410
Ghetto Theresienstadt/Terezín

L410, one of the three Children's Homes in Theresienstadt

HANDA POLLAK

ANNA FLACH

HELGA POLLAK

EVA LANDÁ

MARTA FRÖLICH

JUDITH SCHWARTZBART

HANKA WERTHEIMER

ELA STEIN

VERA NATH

MARIANNA ROSENZWEIG

EVA WINKLER

Editor's note:
The following text is contributed by Hannelore Wonschick, editor of *The Girls from Room 28* (Unpublished manuscript)
Excerpts from her interviews are individually attributed. Translation by Ian Pepper.

The children of Theresienstadt represented the future of Jewish culture. The Ghetto's Self-Government's greatest concern was the moral and intellectual development of the youth. Every effort was made to protect and nourish them. Adults sacrificed portions of their rations so the children were better fed. Children's homes were established—L413/414, the home for youth; L417, in the former school building; and the girls' home, L410 in the former camp headquarters in the market square. Children were housed by year of birth in different rooms, also called "Heime." Male and female guardians, were assigned to each room. Some "room leaders" were highly educated. Many were teachers or artists. They were expected to mentor and care for the children, and to teach them values to prepare them for later life—life after the war.

"There is only one way to remove all negative and destructive aspects from the lives of the young. All educators are obliged to show children so much beauty and truth so there is no longer room in a child's soul for hideousness and falsehood. . . provide [the children] intellectual nourishment, lead them to new knowledge. . . [with] an enormous amount of imagination and thought, stimulate the child to gain new perceptions—all of these things can only be achieved by artists and educators."[1]

Education was thus raised to the level of art at Theresienstadt. "Education is art and art is education," wrote Berta Freund, in a report for the first anniversary of L417, the boy's home. She follows: "We like to say that education is art, in which case the teacher must naturally be an artist. However, he or she need not be a creator of art or an author or be a master of some other art form. He or she is dealing with a much more sensitive substance than many artists deal with—the intellectual and spiritual life of the pupil. To teach the pupil to experience harmony and form in this fashion: this is how the teacher must become an artist. The teacher must awaken the enthusiasm for what is beautiful and noble. This is only possible by the teacher as an artist."[2]

Testimonies of many former inmates of Ghetto Theresienstadt affirm there was no lack of such "artists of pedagogy." Teachers there included Walter Eisinger, Rosa Engländer, Rudolf Freudenfeld, Fredy Hirsch, Ota Klein, Margit Mühlstein, Ella Pollak, Gonda Redlich, Kamilla Rosenbaum, Laura Simková, Eva Weiss and Zdenka Brumlick.

Ten survivors from the group of "Friedl's Girls" reunited in 1989 after the borders opened. They shared memories of childhood, family, and Theresienstadt/Terezín, and decided to write a book about their experiences. Excerpts of their memoirs follow.

Ella Pollak "Tella"
Leader of Room 28

Lenka Lindt
Collage
Born March 19, 1930
Deported to Terezín
February 15, 1942
Deported to Auschwitz
October 28, 1944
Perished
The Jewish Museum, Prague
#121.836

l-r; Handa Pollak, Lenka Lindt

EVA WINKLER ZOHAR

"The unofficial symbol of Room 28 was a flag with the image of two hands in a tight grip, the *Maagal*. Inspired by our room leader, Tella Pollak, we formed the *Maagal*, which meant "circle," and metaphorically, "perfection." To become a member of the *Maagal* was a special honor. Tella strongly influenced us. She taught us to distinguish between bad and good. She first thought of the symbolic *Maagal*. All girls who acted on behalf of the common whole were admitted to this *Maagal*. I believe this was a lovely idea. Each one tried to help others and to be kind to them. To enter the *Maagal*, we tried to be good, tolerant, considerate, orderly, and clean— we strived for perfection."

HANDA POLLAK

"In our room, we were divided for classes in three groups, according to our level of knowledge. We had lessons every morning, but they were always strained, because transports were coming and going all the time. One day we had a teacher who was able to teach us English, so we learned English. The next day he was gone, transported 'to the East.' The teacher who would be found to replace him could teach us mathematics, so we learned mathematics. We learned like this. There was no possibility to keep some plan of learning because everything was so unstable. New pupils arrived, old friends departed. Our teachers came and went. We learned whatever we could. After the war, when I took the exam for the Gymnasium, it turned out that I learned much more than the girls who were able to stay in school during the German occupation of Prague. So I was able to attend the same class where I belonged, with others of my age.

"I believe the reason for me being a tolerant person, how I learned to respect the different convictions of others, and become a good friend, has to do with Room 28 in Theresienstadt. We lived there in a small room, about thirty of us, all with different social backgrounds. Some were spoiled, some were quarrelsome, some egoistic, some were good and others less good, as it happens in life, because each person's character is different. We learned to get along, to listen to one another. We learned to live with each other because there was no way out."

LENKA LINDT

"One is born into the world to do good. Whoever does otherwise has no right to be a human being. If you wish to do what as human beings we must, then do what Tella taught us. Remember always what Tella would have done in your place. I believe that Tella was the most unshakeable person I have known. Remember this my dear friend."

Prior to boarding the transport "to the East," on October 15, 1944, Lenka wrote this good-bye

Reproduction of *Maaghal* flag, with a fragment of the original on lower right.

When a group of the girls from Room 28 were deported to "to the East," they tore the flag into quarters, vowing to reunite it when they met after the war. Only one piece survived.

*Collection of
Anna Flach-Hanusová*

† "Tella" combines the Czech word for "aunt," *teta*, and "Ella."

66

Eva Landa

to Anna Flach ("Flaska") in Flaska's "Memory Book." Lenka Lindt was fourteen. She perished shortly after her arrival in Auschwitz.

EVA LANDA

"When I think of those truly terrible years of the war and the Holocaust, there is a single point of light—our children's residence in the ghetto, our Room 28. I was in Theresienstadt for eighteen months. That's not very long in the life of an adult. But in the life of a child only twelve years old, it's almost eternity. I arrived at Theresienstadt an eleven-year-old girl. When I left the town, in December of 1943, on a transport bound for Auschwitz, I felt like an adult.

"In those hard times, Tella Pollak and Eva Weiss were a great help to us. They taught us a new ideal of humanity, friendship, and solidarity. We received a new scale of values from them, a new conception of human worth. No one could even imagine stealing anything from a fellow resident or neighbor—and if should have happenend once, it was certainly the big exception. All of us, 'the Girls from 28,' strove to realize ourselves, to read more, to know more, to experience more—to improve ourselves.

"We wanted to do good deeds. When the old people arrived on the transports from Germany, we went willingly to help them as best as we could. All we could usually offer

them was a glass of water—those poor old people had been so dreadfully deceived. Many of them had been told that they were traveling to Bad Theresienstadt, a health resort. When they arrived at the ghetto, many simply refused to recognize the atrocious reality.

"Study in the ghetto was strictly forbidden by the Germans. But we studied just the same! There were no textbooks, no notebooks. A piece of paper or a pencil counted as rare luxuries. We also painted often, instructed by Friedl Dicker-Brandeis. In the evenings, our guardians read to us—I don't know how many good books aloud to us by candlelight. There were Czech authors, Jirásek and Čapek, and classics of world literature such as Victor Hugo's *Les Miserables*.

"We had to wash every day with cold water in an unheated washroom, our dishes had to be cleaned, our beds aired out at the window by

Erika Stranská
Collage
Born May 22, 1930
Deported to Terezín
September 4, 1942
Deported to Auschwitz
May 18, 1944
Perished
The Jewish Museum, Prague
#131.942

67

turns. That's how our guardians raised us, how they looked after our physical health. We also had to eat correctly and with good manners, and as far as circumstances allowed, in a healthy way.

"I had good friends in Theresienstadt. My best girlfriends in those days were Handa Pollak and Lenka Lindt. We slept together on a plank bed, and we always got along very well. I admired Lenka for her strong character and her literary talent—she composed beautiful poems. If Lenka had lived, she would have become a great personality. Recently, I bought a pupil's notebook in Prague, and by chance, that contained two poems by Lenka. Both were dedicated to me! She had written them in Theresienstadt, when I was already in Auschwitz-Birkenau.

"Many of us, as Jewish children, had never seen a play or a film before the war. The theater in Ghetto Theresienstadt was something absolutely extraordinary to us! My favorite was the children's opera *Brundibár*, although I was disappointed when I didn't get the role of the student who throws his notebook into the air. I especially loved the finale—the audience always sang the Victory Song with full hearts.

"After the performance, as we turned toward home, and for a while afterwards, we gathered fresh hope that the real Brundibár would soon be defeated. It was clear to all of us, of course, who that meant.

Eva Landa
Pencil on paper
Born December 25, 1930
Deported to Terezín
July 2, 1942
Deported to Auschwitz
December 15, 1943
Survived
The Jewish Museum, Prague
#131.814

"We looked forward with the greatest enthusiasm to collective evenings with the boys from Room 9 of Residence L 417. There were poetry readings, mainly of ballads by the communist poet Jiři Wolker, whose naive communism we felt very close to. His poetry still sounds in my ears, even though I haven't heard or seen any of his poems since then.

"Like all normal children, we loved fun and humor. We laughed from our hearts, when our guardians composed a funny poem about one of us and recited it to us! Or when our girls Lenka Lindt and Anna Flach performed, with such sparkling talent, scenes about two old spinsters, Amalka and Posinka.

"Of course, things in the ghetto were not as happy or cheerful as I've described them. But

Ela Stein

68

Terezín coat-of-arms made by Ela Stein (Weissberger) for Mother's Day, 1944. Using a scrap found in the carpentry shop, located in the basement of L410, Ela burned the design into the wood with a magnifying glass.

thanks to our children's residence, we had something resembling a normal life, even if only slightly—study, reading, painting, play and sport, camaraderie, friendship, and something like young love.

"One day—it was the eleventh of November—the entire population of the ghetto had to be counted, which meant that everyone had to stand waiting in Bauschowitz Hollow for an entire day, surrounded by armed SS-men. Many people became ill. There were terrible infectious diseases in the ghetto—typhus, polio, jaundice, encephalitis. Our home was fortunate. None of our girls died, and no one caught typhus or polio.

"Shortly after, in December 1943, I got encephalitis. I was taken from the hospital and put on a transport heading east. Parting from the children's home was so painful. Our community was formed with so much effort . But I took my memories of our common striving for a better, more just world . I wanted to be—I had to be brave—so as not to betray our ideals. This helped me to overcome hardships. Sadly, only fifteen of the girls from 'Room 28' remain alive.

"Although we live today in different parts of the world, 'the Girls of Room 28' who survived are very close to one another. We've remained good friends, although each of us has a life behind her which was far from easy.

"The Theresienstadt Hymn goes: 'With a will, everything is possible. Let us join hands, and soon we will laugh over the ghetto's ruins.' No one was able to laugh at the ruins of the ghetto, but we remember our childhood in the children's home in 'Room 28' with some affection."

ELA STEIN

"One day, we learned from Tella that the children's opera *Brundibár* was going to be performed. Tella chose several girls, sending us to the loft of the school in L417 for casting. Baštík (Rudolf Freudenfeld) and Rafi (Rafael Schächter) were there, and they told us to sing scales. Our voices trembled with excitement. We were nervous about who would receive which role. We knew that Pinta (Emmanuel Mühlstein) would sing the role of Pepiček, and Greta Hoffmeister that of Aninka. Then Bastik said to me: 'You shall be the Cat.' Since then, he never called me anything else. Even after the war, when he was my teacher in Prague, he just called me 'Kitty-Cat,' which naturally made people wonder a bit.

"When Baštík began rehearsing *Brundibár* with us, it wasn't easy, keeping all of us children in line, but he had incredible patience. Honza Treichlinger, an orphan from Pilsen, got the role of Brundibár, the organ-grinder. He had prayed to receive this part, and he was very

good. No one besides him ever played the
role of Brundibár.

"We awaited the premiere impatiently. Finally,
it took place in the small theater of the
Magdeburg Barracks. When the people filed
into the auditorium, we were all seized with
stage fright. But when the first beat of the
music sounded, we quickly got over it, and
forgetting entirely where we were. As the
opera drew to its close, and we sang the
finale, *Brundibár porazen* ("Brundibár is
defeated"), there was—each time—
thunderous applause which lasted so long
that we almost had to be ejected from the
hall. We were happy, and so was audience.
We all wanted to completely exhaust that
moment of freedom. When we were on stage,
it was the only time we were allowed to
remove our yellow stars.

"I sang fifty-five times in *Brundibár*. I wouldn't allow
a single evening to get away from me. As a
reward for each performance, we received a
little piece of dumpling, a type of pastry, with
a bit of a dark creme in it. Occasionally, Rudi
Freudenfeld's father, the former director
of the Prague orphanage, attended the
performance. Afterwards he would hold me
on his lap and chat. That meant a great deal

Ruth Gutmann
Pencil on paper
Born April 13, 1930
Deported to Terezín
January 17, 1942
Deported to Auschwitz
October 6, 1944
Perished
The Jewish Museum, Prague
#133.007

to me. All of them—Baštik, Kamilla
Rosenbaum, František Zelenka, Hans Krása—
were very concerned for us. We felt loved.

"The songs of *Brundibár* could be heard frequently
in Room 28. Most of the girls in Room 28
sang in the children's choir: Flaska, Maria,
Martha, Handa, Lenka, Zaijèek, Eva, Judith."

Ela Stein (Weissberger) continues to participate in
performances of *Brundibár*, and is active as a
speaker on Holocaust education.

ANNA FLACH (FLASKA)

"So many world-famous artists were there in
Theresienstadt. I attended the concerts of
Alice Sommer-Herz. She once played all of
Chopin's études, which made such a strong
impression on me that I decided one evening
to become a pianist. And that is what I did."

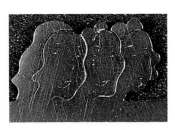

Pin made of "the trio,"
bought with bread:
Ela Stein, Anna Flach,
and Maria Mühlstein

Art, Music and Education as Strategies for Survival: Theresienstadt 1941–45

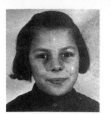

l–r; Anna Flach,
Ruth Schächter "Zajièek"

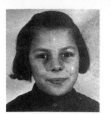

Anna Flach
Pencil on paper
Born November 26, 1931
Deported to Terezín
December 2, 1942
Survived
The Jewish Museum, Prague
#133.417r

Flaska became a pianist, singer, and professor of music at the Conservatory in Brno in the Czech Republic.

While in Theresienstadt Flaska kept a *Gedenkbuch* "Memory Book." It looks, at first glance, like the journals kept by many young girls, with aphorisms, drawings, pressed flowers, and dedications. But many of its inscriptions are parting words of vanished friends.

"Dear Flaska,
I must say goodbye to you today. But we must remain courageous because we have no choice. I hope to see you again somewhere. I also hope that we stay the friends we are. I will think of you each day, and if possible I will write you right away. . . when I sign my name with "Milka," it means that we are being treated badly. But when I sign my name with "Your Miluschka," it means that we are doing well. . . I wish you much luck so that you will have a carefree life. . . think of me and don't forget me. . . live well and remember your dear Miluschka."

Marta Fröhlich
(deported to Auschwitz, survived)

"Remember the one who wrote this and who loved you dearly. Your. . . "— follows is a drawing of a rabbit with seven small baby rabbits, drawn by "Zajièek," Ruth Schächter.

"Zajièek was "'the favorite'" in Room 28. We all loved this little girl who was so grateful for each kind word and who always sought our protection. Due to her large protruding teeth we gave her the nickname 'Zajièek,' which means "bunny." Her parents had fled to Palestine in an illegal transport and had left her and her older brother in an orphanage in Brno. They had no choice. Of course, they hoped to have both children join them soon with the help of a special certificate, but to no avail. Alex and Zajièek, with all the other children in the Brno orphanage were taken to Theresienstadt. And from there to Auschwitz. On May 18, 1944, Zajicèek was ordered onto one of the cattle cars that left Theresienstadt for some eastern destination. Milka had left earlier, on December 14, 1943. On October 16, 1944, Eva Fischl, Maria Mühlstein and many of our others friends from Room 28 were also sent away."

Ruth Schächter "Zaijèek"
Collage
Born April 13, 1930
Deported to Terezín
January 17, 1942
Deported to Auschwitz
October 6, 1944
Perished

The Jewish Museum, Prague
#129.738

72

HANKA WERTHEIMER

"In the children's home we were protected. We never saw everything that really happened in Theresienstadt. At that age, children can easily be distracted by songs and games and all kinds of activities, but older people sometimes cannot. In our 'home,' Room 28, we were able to learn, draw pictures, read books, and talk a lot. We made plans for the future. What I enjoyed most were the long evenings, when we would lie on our hard boards, in darkness. While most children were sleeping, some of us were awake and wondered how soon the war would be over, how we would return home and start a normal life. We agreed to meet again one day once the peace had been announced, on Staroměstske Namesti (Old Town Square) in Prague at noon, right in front of the clock tower. We were still children and had no idea what lay ahead. We were naive, which was our good fortune.

"I often think of Room 28. Today, as a grown woman with three sons, I understand how difficult it must have been for those who cared for us to bring us up well, and to teach us to maintain our personal hygiene, to value friendship, to respect our elders. Although times were very difficult, our guardians made every effort to attained their objectives. We helped the old people; we shared the virtue of honesty, and our friendships with one another were very strong.

"Since I worked most of the time in the garden, I rarely took part in lessons. But I do remember Mrs. Brumlick. She taught Geography and History. I also remember how afraid we were, because lessons were forbidden. We knew that if we were caught, we would be punished.

"I can see it as if it were in front of me—most of the girls lay on their stomachs on their plankbeds, turned towards the center of the room. Each girl had, I think, a notebook, or at least a piece of paper and pencil. Outside, someone would stand watch, giving a sign should the Germans approach the building. The alarm was given several times, and each time, someone quickly gathered all of our things together, bringing them up to the attic. But each time, it was false alarm. I don't remember the SS officers ever actually checking on us. But I certainly remember how afraid we were.

"We also sketched with Friedl Brandeis. We were given lessons by individuals of the highest

Ela Stein
June 30, 1930
Deported to Terezín
February 12, 1942
Survived
The Jewish Museum, Prague
#129.434

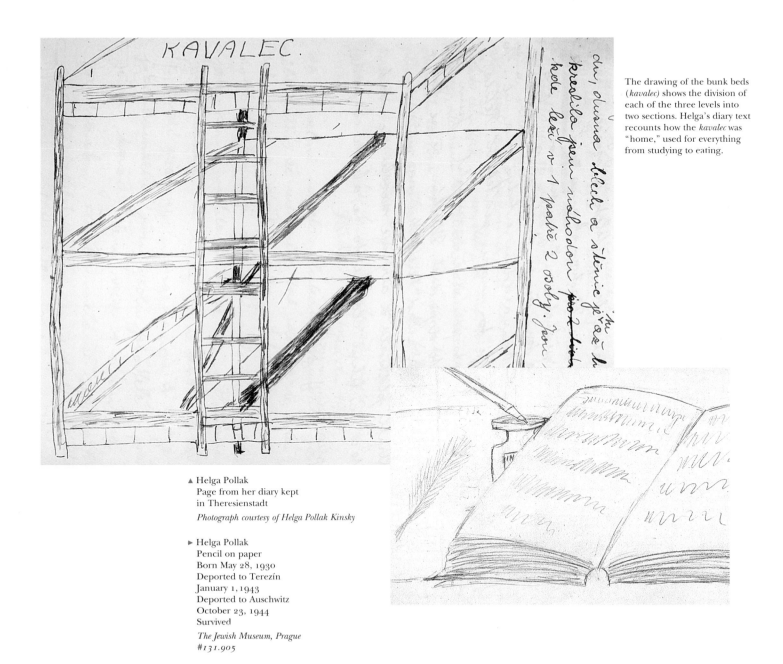

KAVALEC.

The drawing of the bunk beds (*kavalec*) shows the division of each of the three levels into two sections. Helga's diary text recounts how the *kavalec* was "home," used for everything from studying to eating.

▲ Helga Pollak
Page from her diary kept
in Theresienstadt
Photograph courtesy of Helga Pollak Kinsky

▶ Helga Pollak
Pencil on paper
Born May 28, 1930
Deported to Terezín
January 1, 1943
Deported to Auschwitz
October 23, 1944
Survived
The Jewish Museum, Prague
#131.905

Art, Music and Education as Strategies for Survival: Theresienstadt 1941–45

74

▲ Irena Grünfeld
Pencil on paper
Born October 15, 1930
Deported to Terezín
June 13, 1942
Deported to Auschwitz
December 15, 1943
Perished

The Jewish Museum, Prague
#129.118

◄ Hanna Lissau
Collage
Born February 4, 1930
Deported to Terezín
February 25, 1942
Deported to Auschwitz
October 16, 1944
Perished

The Jewish Museum, Prague
#131.875

Helga Pollak
Pencil on paper
Born May 28, 1930
Deported to Terezín
January 1, 1943
Deported to Auschwitz
October 23 1944
Survived

The Jewish Museum, Prague
#131.908r

caliber. Such people would never have taught in a normal Czech elementary school. But there in Theresienstadt, we were taught by professors, all of them quite extraordinary."

HELGA POLLAK

"I remember so clearly our drawing lessons from Friedl Dicker-Brandeis. What a wonderful artist she was! I can still see the table in the middle of the room with pencils on it, paintbrushes, colors, and paper. The paper was very poor quality, often waste paper or paper left over from some old package.

"I believe there were no restrictions. Each child could draw freely according to its imagination and wishes. This was extraordinary. It gave us a different life, another atmosphere. It was then and there when my love of art and of things of beauty began. I never lost this love of art.

"Mrs. Brandeis was a small, fidgety woman, but very nice. We had great respect for her. She had short hair, light-brown, I believe, a rather pale face, and she was of small stature. She always brought her materials with her, paper, paint, sometimes a small object for us to paint. At the end of each lesson, one of the girls would volunteer to help carry her things back downstairs. When she chose me, I was very proud.

"Sometimes she brought various papers, and I would make collages. We often painted the

Unknown Child Artist
Collage
The Jewish Museum, Prague
#131.872r

Studies from Bartolomeo da Veneto, (1502–46), *Weibliches Brusbild*, cited by Elena Makarova in *vom Bauhaus nach Terezín*, (Frankfurt:1991) *ii*

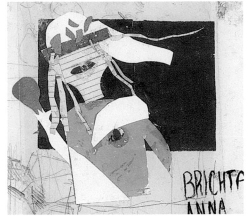

Anna Brichtá
Collage
Born February 24, 1930
Deported to Terezín July 27, 1942
Deported to Auschwitz May 15, 1944
Perished
The Jewish Museum, Prague
#131.940r

Bartolomeo da Veneto (1502–46),
Weibiches Brusbild,
Copy courtesy Städeisches Kunstinstitut,
Frankfurt am Main

Chava Winkler

76

▶ Chava Winkler (Eva)
Colored pencil on paper
Born October 12, 1930
Deported to Terezín
April 6, 1942
Survived

The Jewish Museum, Prague
#129.018

▶ Vera Nath
Collage
Born March 25, 1931
Deported to Terezín
December 8, 1942
Survived

The Jewish Museum, Prague
#129.432

collages. We also painted with watercolors or simply sketched. She often brought art books, and I believe, also postcards of works of art, and she had us imitate famous paintings, either with collage or with watercolor. Or she would bring flowers or some other item— some pots or a few wooden shoes. Once she told us to just paint each other, or to paint something that was especially important to us.

"She often gave us specific subjects, assigned themes for us to draw. But she would also tell us to use our free imagination, telling us to just paint the place where you wish you were now. Or to paint what you wish for. Then, of course, each child painted something different.

"You can see certain themes that repeat in our children's drawings, and in those of children from other classes. Everyone enjoyed painting lessons. It wasn't necessary to be able to draw well. That was not the most important thing to Friedl. It was a question of unfolding one's capacities, of learning how to see. To recognize colors. To play with colors. To draw something in relation to music or to a certain rhythm. For instance, she would rap softly on the table, and we had to draw in rhythm to her movements. There was something about her way of teaching that made us feel, for the moment, free of care. She somehow managed to awaken in us a positive attitude about our situation, about living in Theresienstadt."

Marta Fröhlich

MARTA FRÖHLICH

"I had seen some pictures painted by Eva Winkler,
and I was envious. So I said to her: How
lovely. I want to learn to do that, too. Eva
took me along to see Friedl Brandeis, who
lived in a little shed in the courtyard of Block
L410. Friedl had covered her walls with dyed
blue cloth, which had pictures stitched on
it. Sometimes a vase with flowers stood on
her table.

"With Friedl Brandeis, it wasn't only a question of
painting. She always spoke with me,
explaining what was good, what was beautiful.
I remember a lesson with Friedl—I drew
several lines. Then she asked me, 'What do
you suppose you could make out of those
lines?' I don't know, I answered. 'But surely
you see something there!' I don't see
anything, I answered. Friedl said: 'Then we
will just have to turn the page a little bit.' And
she rotated the page. 'Do you see anything
now?' I answered: 'No.' So she rotated the
page again: 'Now?' 'No, not yet.' Then she
said: 'You have looked at one of my picture
book so often. What did you see there? What
did you especially like to look at?' Suddenly,
in my mind's eye, I saw a dancing woman
from the book. So I painted a dancer based
on those lines. Then she said: 'Yes, now I'm
sure: you can see. You have talent. You can
study painting with me.'

**To direct the sparks of children's
inspiration, those sudden
illuminations, is criminal!**

**Why are adults in such a hurry
to make children like themselves?
Are we really so happy and
satisfied with ourselves?**

Friedl Dicker-Brandeis

From a letter to Johannes Itten,
as cited in Elena Makarova,
*From Bauhaus to Terezín,
Friedl Dicker-Brandeis and her Pupils*
(Jerusalem: Yad Vashem, 1990), 6

Marta Fröhlich
Colored pencil
Born July 17, 1928
Deported to Terezín
February 16, 1943
Survived
The Jewish Museum, Prague
#133.548

78

Eva Sternová
Ink on paper
Born October 12, 1930
Deported to Terezín
April 8, 1942
Deported to Auschwitz
October 23, 1944
Survived
The Jewish Museum, Prague
#131.949

"One day Friedl Brandeis said: 'We are going to put on an exhibition. Each student will paint something, and whoever is really good will get something.' I thought it over—what could I make? I wanted to do something in three dimensions. But how? Friedl had some cork, wire, paper, and wool. From these materials, I improvised a sculpture based on my memory of a photograph in one of Friedl's books, of a tree and two monkeys, one standing in front of it, the other hanging from a branch. My sculpture was shown in the exhibit in the cellar of L410. I received first prize for it.

"That was the first time I was the best at anything. I'm still grateful to her for everything she taught me. I learned to look around me with awareness, always to see something new, and to form something out of what I see. She taught me to work with perseverance and conscientiousness, and to finish whatever I had started."

JUDITH SCHWARTZBART

"Our chaperons and teachers were wonderful. How did they manage it so that we not only endured each other, but also helped one another? That we studied willingly, kept the room neat and clean, and washed our hair, although it was very unpleasant. Handling about thirty girls between the difficult age of twelve and fourteen years living in one single room together! Today I realize that Tella accomplished something extraordinary—

Judith Schwartzbart

although she wasn't liked by everyone, because she was very strict. Today I can see that it was no easy task, keeping all of us girls reasonably peaceful under such terrible circumstances, surrounded by hunger, illness, homesickness—not to mention the constant fear of transport.

"We were always terrified of new transports. Continually. When we saw people in the street dragging along bags and suitcases, it frightened us terribly. We had no idea where they were going. No one knew what the Germans planned to do with us. The fear was always there.

"Most of us had to join transports. And what came after that was so horrible, that you simply want to forget. For in reality, Terezín was a moderate experience compared to that which followed."

VERA NATH

"I do not remember the time in Theresienstadt very well. It is a closed chapter for me. And I never wanted to live in the shadow of the Holocaust. I am convinced that if I had, this would have meant that Hitler won. After the war, I started a new life. I was lucky—my mother, father and sister survived. I came to Room 28 rather late, maybe in December 1943 and lived there till the closure of the 'Girls home,' after the big transports in October 1944. I think I worked in the

◄ Judith Schwartzbart
Watercolor
Born June 2, 1933
Deported to Terezín
March 31, 1942
Deported to Auschwitz
October 19, 1944
Survived
The Jewish Museum, Prague
#135.092

◄ Anna Brichtá
Watercolor
Born February 24, 1930
Deported to Terezín
July 27, 1942
Deported to Auschwitz
May 15, 1944
Perished
The Jewish Museum, Prague
#131.844

80

Pages from Vera Nath's
Terezín scrapbook
Courtesy of Vera Nath Kreiner

garden, so I was not in the room that much, that might be why I was not as close friends as were the other girls. And I had my parents and my sister in Terezín whom I visited quite often.

"I remember, though, the muscial life in Terezín. My brother-in-law, Jirka Steiner; was active in the *Freizeitgestaltung*. He played the flute and performed with different chamber ensembles. So I visited quite a lot of performances whereever they took place, very often in the attics. The most lasting impression was made on me by the pianist Alice Sommer-Herz, when she played all Chopin's études. That was really something. And of course I remember *Brundibár*.

"What is very important for me, which came out of my coming of age during the war is that when I had children I wanted them to never have to change schools. I wanted them not to be torn away from what was familiar to them. I wanted them to not constantly have to change their friends. This was a terrible thing in Terezín, when friends that you just won disappear one day to another. And never show up again."

MARIANNA ROSENZWEIG

"Living in L 410 was actually a great privilege. We
were not supposed to learn, but we did. I
made many drawings. It is interesting that
even though we were very young and suffered
hunger, cold and fear, we always stayed very
honest and decent. We all had very strong
morales, just as we were taught at home.

"I think that the time in Room 28 was the best
time that I spent in Terezin, a time that was
much easier than the others, a time when I
was with girls of my own age in a room, where
we slept on bunkbeds, and not on the floor.
The time in Room 28 was much better than
all the other times I went through during the
time that I was in the ghetto and the
concentration camp.

"One thing about all those terrible years of the
war—I realize that many people might
remember different things than I do, but I
don't remember one occasion when one of us
stole anything from the other. We developed
very very strong friendships, something that is
very difficult, I think, to find under normal
circumstances. I don't dwell too much on the
past. But as the youngest of us are getting old,
I feel as many others do—that our past
should not be forgotten. For many years we
did not talk about our war experiences, but
now it is time. We must speak before it is
too late."

Ruth Guttman
Collage
Born April 13, 1930
Deported to Terezín
January 17, 1942
Deported to Auschwitz
October 6, 1944
Perished
The Jewish Museum, Prague
#129.755

NOTES

1. Berta Freund, "Erziehung ist Kunst, Kunst ist Erziehung," as
cited in *Theresienstädter Studien und Dokumente* (Prague, 1998), 163
2. Ibid. Berta Freund, an educator, was deported to Theresienstadt
on December 2, 1942 from Brünn. She was transported to
Auschwitz on October 9, 1944, where she perished.

Hannelore Wonschick and Anne D. Dutlinger

Nepřežil bych, kdyby nebylo kamarádství.

If not for friendship, I would not have survived.

"The Girls from Room 28" reunite at a conference on *Brundibár* organized by Jeunesse Musicales in Weikersheim, Germany, April 1999

l–r, foreground: Marta Fröhlich, Chava Winkler, Ela Stein
back row: Judith Schwartzbart, Vera Nath, Helga Pollak, Anna Flach (Flaska), Eva Landa, Handa Pollak, Hanka Wertheimer

Photograph courtesy of Ela Stein Weissberger

"THE GIRLS" FROM ROOM 28

HANNA BRADY

MARIANNA DEUTSCH

HANNA EPSTEIN

EVA FISCHL

ANNA FLACH

MARTA FRÖHLICH

RUTH GUTTMANN

IRENA GRÜNFELD

EVA HELLER

MARTA KENDE

EVA KOHN

EVA LANDA

LENKA LINDT

HANNA LISSAU

OLGA LÖWY

ZDENKA LÖWY

RUTH MAISL

HELENA MÄNDL

MARIA MÜHLSTEIN

VERA NATH

MILKA POLLÁCEK

HANDA POLLAK

HELGA POLLAK

RUTH POPPER

MARIANNA ROSENZWEIG

RUTH SCHÄCHTER

JUDITH SCHWARTZBART

PAVLA SEINER

ALICE SITTIG

JIRINA STEINER

ELA STEIN

EVA STERN

ERICA STRÁNSKÁ

EMMA TAUB

ZUZANA WEISSKOPF

HANKA WERTHEIMER

EVA WINKLER

BOLDFACE TYPE INDICATES GIRLS FROM ROOM 28 WHO SURVIVED

Theresienstadt will be of no use to us if later in life we oppress even one single human being.

Margit Mühlstein
L 410
Nurse and caretaker

Alice Sittig
Pencil on paper
Born April 19, 1930
Deported to Terezín
April 9, 1942
Deported to Auschwitz
May 18, 1944
Perished

The Jewish Museum, Prague
 # 133.013

The things one accomplishes after intense work and succeeds in doing for many reasons, are usually good. The more objectively one works, the happier one is, but the big things...are the engines that get everything going; the paralyzing dimensions are the ones that call one from play to order....

I have just slipped through the net and am grateful and happy to be alive. I only hope that should I one day have to pay for this, that I will have saved up enough strength to be able to do this. Here you have my likeness in the car. You can see how extremely resolute she is. [1]

Friedl Dicker-Brandeis
Letter to Hilde Kothny
December 9, 1940

Friedl Dicker-Brandeis
Lady in a Car (Self-portrait)
Pastel on paper
43.5 x 56 cm
1940
The Jewish Museum, Prague
#176.282

MICHAELA HÁJKOVÁ

Friedl Dicker-Brandeis wrote these words in 1940 from her home in Hronov, a small provincial town in eastern Bohemia, to her closest friend, Hilde Kothny. Four years later Dicker-Brandeis vanished in the gas chambers at Auschwitz-Birkenau.

When Dicker-Brandeis wrote her letter, in the snug world of the Czech countryside, it must have been very difficult for her to imagine absolute nothingness. On the contrary, Friedl Dicker-Brandeis lived there because the small everyday affairs served to fill the void. Judging from several of her letters to friends written from there, Hronov was the only place where she found a sense of home, harmony, and, in a way, a perfect though short-lived happiness.

Home—what is it exactly? Was it Vienna, where Friedl-Dicker was born and raised? Was "home" in the cities where she studied art or later worked, in small-town Weimar or cosmopolitan Berlin? Was it in Prague,[2] to which she fled as a refugee in 1934?

Friedl Dicker-Brandeis was born on July 30, 1898, into a Viennese middle-class family, the only child of Simon and Karoline Dicker (née Fanta). Her mother died when she was three years old, her father was left to raise her alone. In 1903, a photograph was taken of Simon Dicker, a paper goods merchant, roughly forty years old at the

Friedl Dicker-Brandeis
c. 1936
*Copy courtesy
The Jewish Museum, Prague*

time, with his young daughter, Friedl, It was photographed at the studio of Strauss on Mariahilferstrasse in Vienna. She is somewhat timidly holding on to the lapels of his best suit. Yet, still a small child, she boldly turns her fastidiously beribboned head toward the camera and directs a plucky, piercing look, along with her pursed lips, and conveys a strong determination.

Reflecting on photography years later, she expressed a good deal of skepticism: "A photograph is an excerpted moment in time. . . . Photos cannot reveal anything, since it is impossible for them to convey—in the blink of an eye—the relationship between individuals and their surroundings or to each other."[3]

Friedl Dicker's rejection of photography as an inadequate form of copying reality was already apparent in her early studies as a student of the Graphische Lehr und Versuchsanstalt in Vienna, where she had enrolled with her father's support.[4] Friedl Dicker believed that black-and-white photography did not provide her with enough artistic freedom. Her rejection of a career in photography enabled her, at seventeen years old, to initiate her own path in art education.

In 1915 Friedl Dicker enrolled as a student in the textile department of the Vienna School of Applied Arts, attending the class taught by

Friedl Dicker with
with her father, Simon
Vienna 1903
*Copy courtesy
private collection*

A class of students in
Franz Čížek's school

Unknown Child Artist
*(Artwork by a student in
Franz Čížek's school)*
Cut paper and collage

Photographs by J. Bohl
Both images cited from
Wilhelm Viola, *Child Art
and Franz Čížek*, (Vienna
Austrian International
Red Cross, 1936)

Rosalie Rothansl. She also began to attend
Franz Čížek's course.[5] In Čížek's class she
first encountered the progressive teaching
method associated with the theory of
ornamental forms—*ornamentale Formenlehre*.
This "ornamental course," as it was
sometimes called, was both controversial
and influential. Its methods and philosophy
were part of the introductory course at the
Bauhaus taught by Johannes Itten.[6]

In 1916, young Friedl transferred to Itten's private
school in Vienna soon after it opened. Two
years later she followed Itten, now her
mentor, to the Bauhaus in Weimar, where he
had been invited to relocate in 1919 by the
school's new director, Walter Gropius.[7] Friedl
Dicker was not the only student to follow or
venerate Itten. Johannes Itten was
charismatic, a guru with a smoothly shaven
head and an advocate of vegetarianism and
eastern mysticism. He attracted students who
became intensely connected with one another
under his tutelage and formed lifelong
collaborations and friendships.

Before leaving for Weimar, Friedl Dicker became
friends with fellow classmates Margit Téry and
Anny Wottitz (later Moller), but she was
closest to Franz Singer. She was attached to
him not only because of their close working
relationship, but also by a strong emotional
bond. After Singer's marriage to Emmy
Heim, her relationship with Franz Singer
turned into a painful love affair.

Friedl Dicker then coped with the loneliness of the
outsider—not for the first or last time in her
life. Her relationship with Singer was a
tangled thread running through her whole
life, and apparently the cause of Dicker's
inability to settle down and lead a quiet life,
to give her full attention to her work and
have a family. She confides feelings of
loneliness in one of her letters to her close
friend and colleague Anny Wottitz: "Dearest
Anny, a great fear of solitude, of myself alone,
has come over me. God willing, I'll get
through it."[8]

She tried to offset her personal disappointment by
working constantly at a feverishly intense
pace; the Bauhaus provided her with nearly

ideal conditions for this. She had the opportunity to visit the separate ateliers, learn different techniques, and acquire experience with a variety of materials and media. For someone as versatile and gifted as Friedl Dicker, the Bauhaus was paradise. She created typography for Itten's almanac, *Utopia*, and the design for the invitations to "Bauhaus culture evenings"; she designed book bindings, worked in the textile workshop run by Georg Muche,[9] and the printing workshop under the direction of Lyonel Feininger.[10] She also spent time in the atelier for sculpture run by Oskar Schlemmer,[11] who in 1923 took over the atelier for stage design. Friedl Dicker had been fascinated with theater since childhood, and Schlemmer's work inspired her, so she collaborated with Franz Singer on a number of design proposals for the German experimental directors Lothar Schreyer, Berthold Viertel, and later, Bertolt Brecht.

It was Itten's course, however, that provided Friedl Dicker with preparation for her later work as an important artist and teacher. In class, Itten developed his method of instruction, the rudiments of which he had borrowed from his teacher, Adolf Hölzel[12] in Stuttgart. Emphasis was placed on the elementary discipline of forms, color, and rhythm—the mastering of these fundamentals by means of *hell-dunkel Studien* (studies of light and shadow), color compositions, rhythmic

If I want to feel and live a line, I must move my hand along the path of that line. I must follow that line with my senses, that is, I must move in my soul. Then I will finally be able to sense that line spiritually, to see it, then I will move in spirit.

Johannes Itten
as cited in Elena
Makarova, *From Bauhaus
to Terezin: Friedl Dicker-
Brandeis and Her Pupils*
(Jerusalem, 1990), 4

Gabi Frei
Pencil on paper
Born January 1, 1933
Deported to Terezín
December 9, 1942
Deported to Auschwitz
May 18, 1944
Perished
The Jewish Museum, Prague
#129.950

Friedl Dicker
Three Ducks
Lithograph on paper
c. 1920
Collection of Georg Schrom

Friedl Dicker-Brandeis
Still Life
Charcoal, n.d.
*Simon Wiesenthal
Museum of Tolerance,
Los Angeles*

drawing exercises based on the transposition of acoustic perception to graphic form, and, finally, analysis of classical works of art.[13]

This process was designed to assist the students in achieving a total release of their creative energy, resulting in an entirely new and original work: original in the sense that one is divested of everything that does not arise from experience, as well as that which serves merely superficial communication rather than the ultimate objective of self-expression.

The quest for pure expression is connected with the quest for pure form and color and their application in the framework of *Gesamtkunstwerk*, in which each of the work's elements is integrated into a harmonious form. This method is perhaps best illustrated by Friedl Dicker's interior sculpture, *St. Anne,*[14] which she executed in 1920 and 1921. From the first sketches for this work one can see the effort taken to achieve a harmonious order through purity of color and clearly articulated composition. The sculpture has its own well-defined, logical ordering of cylindrical forms. The compactness and verticality of the composition also suggests the sacred character of medieval sculpture.

Interestingly, a similar delineated sequence of "generations" can be traced in some of the children's drawings, the principles of which Dicker later studied intensively.[15] At the same

Friedl Dicker
Landscape with a Lake
Charcoal on paper,
31.5 x 43.5 cm
c. 1920–23
The Jewish Museum, Prague
#176.276

František Brozan
Pencil on paper, 19.5 x 24 cm
Born December 13, 1932
Deported to Terezín
November 13, 1942
Deported to Auschwitz
December 15, 1944
Perished
The Jewish Museum, Prague
#129.411r

time, the forms in *St. Anne,* positions the work in a subordinate role in relation to the space for which it was created: the villa of Auguste and Hilda Heriot.[16] The sculpture is wedged into a corner of a mezzanine by a stairwell, which suggests a reference to principles of cathedral architecture. The sculpture-column loosely paraphrases this principle. But rather than the sculpture's crown being contiguous with the structural rib that would support the weight of the vault, there is an open space between the crown and the ceiling's glass center, as if the angel above St. Anne's head had flown down through the space above.

At first glance it appears paradoxical that the figure of the angel does not have wings and has therefore been stripped of its most basic attribute. From the perspective of St. Anne iconography, the mere presence of this angel, an allusion to the Immaculate Conception, is an entirely incongruous element. This explicitly articulated departure from tradition renders the originally marginal and subordinate components—as an interior sculpture within the context of *Gesamt-kunstwerk*—as a wholly organic work, an unqualified *Andachtsbild*, an image meeting the standards of purely conceptual work.

There is more here than just Dicker's fascination with the image of mother and child. A combination of personal themes and conceptual thinking results in an exceptionally powerful work. Indeed, the art historian Hans Hildebrandt [17] has called it one of the most original works by a woman in all of modern art.

Friedl Dicker frequently returned to the motif of mother and child, the basis for which is the traditional iconography of the Madonna. Mention should be made here of the drawings; *Mother Nursing Her Child*, [18] *Hanna Deutsch as an Infant*, [19] and the painting *Gypsy Woman with Child*, [20] in which Dicker depicts an extreme state of exaltation, through contrast between the pallor of the dead child and the swarthy complexion of the mother.

During the period Friedl Dicker spent in Weimar (1919–23), one cannot overlook the enormous influence of Paul Klee, [21] both for his versatility as an artist, and his interest in children's drawings. Klee was fascinated by children's creativity, and applied it to his own work. [22] He was not reticent about using iconography from his own childhood. He studied children's drawings in detail, as did many other artists of the classical period of modernism: Vasily Kandinsky, Gabriele Münter, Pablo Picasso, Joan Miró among others. [23] Meeting Paul Klee was clearly a decisive moment in Friedl Dicker's life. From that point on, she engaged in an ongoing, concentrated study of children's artwork.

Friedl Dicker
St. Anne Selbdritt
Studies for sculpture
Watercolor on paper
University of Applied Arts, Vienna , #8701

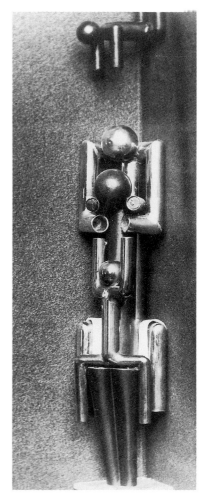

Friedl Dicker
St. Anne Selbdritt
Sculpture created for the home of Auguste and Hilda Heriot, 1921 (Sculpture destroyed)
Bauhaus-Archiv, Berlin

Friedl Dicker
Mother Nursing Her Child
Charcoal on paper,
63 x 45 cm
c. 1931
The Jewish Museum, Prague
#176.183

92

Johannes Itten left the Bauhaus in 1923, as did a number of his students, among them were Friedl Dicker and Franz Singer. In the same year Dicker and Singer opened a studio together in Berlin, giving it the rather prosaic name Werkstätten Bildender Kunst (Fine Arts Workshop). They took a variety of commissions, establishing themselves notably in the area of architectural and interior design, though they also received many offers from the theater world.[24] For Dicker this was a period marked by dynamic work, and despite Singer's marriage, the persistence of a complicated love affair.

Dicker left Berlin in 1925 and moved back to Vienna where she opened a bookbinding and textile design atelier with one of her friends.

But Singer soon followed her there, and together they founded Atelier Singer-Dicker where they produced on commission a number of outstanding designs. The studio's sphere of activity encompassed many of the important Central European cultural centers at that time: Vienna, Budapest, Berlin, Prague, and Brno. Their work was represented and highly praised in numerous exhibitions.[25] In addition to commissions from individuals for the interior design of private homes and apartments, they also took commissions for public buildings. Of particular note were a tennis clubhouse in Vienna (1928) and the nursery school in Vienna's Goethehof (1930). Unfortunately, neither is extant.

After a period of intensive work for the studio, the beginning of the 1930s brought a significant change to Dicker's life. First and foremost, she focused on her own work and what she felt was most important: personal and artistic freedom. Although Atelier Singer-Dicker still formally existed, Dicker also rented her own studio and began to concentrate most of her effort on working with children and art instruction.

This resulted in changes in both her style and choice of subjects in her own work—Dicker began to produce collages as a form of social protest. She created posters reflecting the deteriorating social conditions brought on by the growing economic crisis resulting from the Great Depression, particularly where the lives of children were concerned.

When Hitler came to power in Germany in 1933, Dicker's "committed" art took an even stronger political subtext. She decided to cooperate with the Austrian Communist party that was subsequently banned in February 1934. After Count Starhemberg led a right-wing *putsch* in Austria in February 1934, she was arrested, interrogated, and eventually imprisoned, as a result of her political activities.

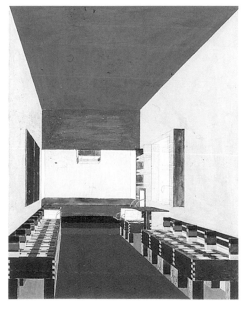

Atelier Singer-Dicker
Garden Room — Hatschek
Perspective drawing
Pencil, colored pencil and
tempera on cardboard
1927
Collection of Georg Schrom

Although her stay in prison was not especially long (she was released the same year), this experience marked an irreversible turning point in her life. Disillusioned and hurt, Dicker decided to leave her native Vienna to seek refuge in Prague. Although she had relatives there, her maternal aunt Adéla Brandeis (née Fanta) and her three sons, it was still a relatively unfamiliar environment. She felt a strong sense of alienation, which is reflected in her correspondence, expressed in a letter to Anny Wottitz shortly after arriving in Prague: "The image of home, the land, is nothing but an image, and we're certainly not idolaters, even if we are uprooted."[26]

During this period Dicker started to form a deeply melancholic image of the world, which was later applied in the drawing, *Lady in a Car*.[27] She likewise drew on her last experiences in Vienna in the paintings, *Interrogation I* and *Interrogation II*, both of which made palpable the vivid nightmares and the persisting depression brought on by the interrogation and the threat to her personal freedom.[28] These paintings also signify her first in-depth observation of her own "I" and her actual situation. For the first time she began to articulate a clear view of herself. She remained strictly detached, which not only enabled her to step outside herself, but also gave her a medium with which she could express her trauma. *Interrogation I* is not a self-

94

Friedl Dicker-Brandeis
Portrait of Vera Sormová
Oil on canvas
49.5 x 71 cm
c. 1936
The Jewish Museum, Prague
#176.285

portrait of the usual type—as are the two drawings made during her studies at Bauhaus.[29] It is a retrospective expression of her being in a situation where her "I" is severely constrained by its surroundings. Evidently this is what she had in mind when she spoke of her distrust of photography as a medium capable of capturing the essence of reality.

Even though Dicker could not accept Prague with its legendary Kafkaesque "claws," as her home, she made a number of good friends there, several of whom were with her almost until the end of her life. After a short time in Prague she grew close to her cousin Pavel Brandeis, whom she married in 1936. Marriage provided some compensation for her painful memories. She took her husband's name, changing "D" to "B" in her signature, and again threw herself into work with characteristic enthusiasm, collaborating on interior designs with her friends in Vienna, and teaching children from a refugee community. During this time, she also produced a series of oil paintings depicting the picturesque scenery along the banks of the Vltava River,[30] and an austere pedestrian view of a street corner under Vyšehrad, in the Nusle district of Prague.[31]

The experience of a new environment and her newly found equilibrium nevertheless did not mean a renewal of her work as an artist to its

Friedl Dicker-Brandeis
Portrait of a Woman in Yellow Sweater
Smoking a Cigarette
Pastel on paper
60 x 45 cm
c. 1938–42
The Jewish Museum, Prague
#176.185

Friedl Dicker
Interrogation I
Oil on plywood
120 x 80 cm
1934/35
The Jewish Museum, Prague
#176.189

fullest extent. In 1938, international political tension was increasing. While calm still prevailed in Prague, refugees continued to flood the city making it clear that elsewhere the political situation was worsening. Job opportunities were becoming increasingly scarce, and life in the city became unbearable. In the summer of 1938, just a few weeks before the "betrayal" at Munich resulting in the German occupation of western Czechoslovakia, the Brandeises decided to move to the small town of Hronov in Eastern Bohemia.

Friedl Dicker's world was gradually shrinking. The anti-Jewish regulations, became more severe day by day.[32] Her world was progressively reduced to minimal living space, a circle of friends, but also, themes for inspiration. For Dicker this meant turning to everyday affairs and to her close friends within reach. The transformation of her world, the harsh experience of internal and ultimately actual emigration, was behind her. She now knew how to orient herself in unfamiliar surroundings, to "inhabit" her world, and utilize its language. Her motivation was provided chiefly by her husband, whom she refused to abandon when she was offered passage to Palestine.

While still in Prague, Friedl Dicker's work had taken on a more somber tone. Her gaze gradually turned to ordinary things. There, well-conceived still life compositions, her drafting precision in modeling shapes, and her economy of color suggested neoclassicism.[33] Color was emphasized in her watercolor and pastel drawings.[34] There is a carefree playfulness that characterizes the drawings of intimately known things and people, and her pastels reflected her enchantment with the tones of the landscape around Hronov. By contrast she utilized subdued and dark tones in her paintings,

Friedl Dicker-Brandeis
Pavel
Pastel on paper
43.3 x 38.5 cm
c. 1940
The Jewish Museum, Prague #176.281

namely, the chiaroscuro-like allegories from the second half of the 1930s and the beginning of the 1940s. Moreover, the diagonal principle of these paintings suggests the baroque compositions of old masters: *The Resurrection of Lazarus*[35] is a direct allusion to Rembrandt and the vaguely named *Don Quixote and Lenin*[36] displays the traditional iconographic schema of the conversion of St. Paul or of St. Martin of Tours giving his cape to a beggar.

At the end of 1942, Dicker received her transport notice. With it came a difficult farewell to a small and intimate world. Friedl and Pavel Brandeis arrived in Terezín on December 17, 1942 on transport Ch from Hradec Králové. Their suitcases were marked with transport numbers 548 and 549.

But the new environment, despite its privations, inspired Dicker-Brandeis. Very soon after her arrival she began to organize drawing classes for the children in their dormitories, tirelessly gathering paper and art supplies, which was far from easy, given conditions in the ghetto. Every scrap of wrapping paper and discarded military forms were used for drawings. The dimensions of Friedl Dicker-Brandeis's outer world were shrinking, but her inner world was growing richer than ever before.

In addition to the excellent art instruction Dicker-Brandeis provided the children in Terezín, she also gave them freedom, an escape from the horrible reality in the ghetto. One possible means of escape was by looking out the window: "A window is there to be looked out of," she was fond of saying. She had always tried to capture what she saw in the opening created by the window frame: in Prague, in Františkovy Lázně, in Hronov, everywhere that offered her a look beyond her gradually contracting world. In Terezín, the pictures she created of the views from the window took on an entirely new dimension.[37] They symbolized an escape into the distance, from the windows in Terezín, one could see beyond the bulwarks, an idyllic landscape—the Czech Central Mountains, the setting sun.

Friedl Dicker-Brandeis was deported from Terezín to Auschwitz-Birkenau on October 6, 1944, eight days after her husband. She was killed in the gas chambers shortly after arrival, accompanied by a group of her young students.

Essay translated
from Czech by
Howard Sidenberg

Terezín had many world famous specialists in every field and most of them were glad to give lessons or seminars for bread. (I was glad to give my bread for this better nourishment!)

But... Friedl was the only one who didn't take a crumb for lessons. She simply gave herself to us.

Erna Furman
From Bauhaus to Terezín: Friedl Dicker-Brandeis and Her Pupils (Jerusalem, 1990), 38

Unknown Child Artist
At the Dormitory Window
Pencil on paper
19.5 x 24 cm, n.d.
The Jewish Museum, Prague
#121.515

Robert Perl
View through a Window
Pastel on paper
20.5 x 29.7 cm
Born June 6, 1932
Deported to Terezín
March 6, 1943
Deported to Auschwitz
October 4, 1944
Perished
The Jewish Museum, Prague
#130.530

If we want to look at children's drawing with pleasure and profit, we must first silence our wishes and requirements about form and content and gratefully take what they have to offer....

The aim is the maximum freedom of the child, their free choice of expression according to their mood.... Everything must be left to the child. At most they should be given a subject, an impulse.

From manuscript notes
by Friedl Dicker-Brandeis
for her lecture on children's
drawing, Theresienstadt, 1943

Arno Pařík, *Friedl Dicker-Brandeis 1898–1944*
(exhibition catalog)
State Jewish Museum,
Prague: 1988

Friedl Dicker-Brandeis
Landscape Still Life
(View from a Window in Hronov)
Oil on pasteboard
61.5 x 49.7 cm
c. 1938–42
The Jewish Museum, Prague
#176.258

NOTES

1. *Die dinge, die man nach dem Angestrengten und aus vielen Motiven Gemachten zu Stande bringt, sind meist die guten. Je unbefangener man arbeitet, desto glückicher, aber die grossen Sachen mit vielen Absichten sind die Motore, die alles in Schwung bringen, die lähmenden Grossen solche, die einen von der Spielerei zur Ordnung rufen. [...] Ich bin eben durchs Netz geschlüpft und freue mich dankbar des Lebens. Ich hoffe nur, sollte ich einmal dafür zahlen müssen, eben daraus soviel Kraft aufgespeichert zu haben, um es zu können. Da hast du meine Frische im "Wagen." Du siehst, wie äusserst determiniert sie ist.* Friedl Dicker-Brandeis in a letter addressed to Hilde Kothny, Hronov, December 9, 1940.

2. *Mir geht es, freundlich gesagt, sehr mässig; aber es wird schon besser. Prag will mir nicht Freund werden.* Excerpt from letter by Friedl Dicker-Brandeis, Prague to her friend and colleague Poldi Schrom, a Viennese architect, 1936.

3. *Die Photographie, Ausschnitt eines Augenblicks. [...] Sie sagt aus, dass nichts auszusagen ist. Denn die Beziehung der Menschen zur Umwelt und zu sich selbst kann in einem Augenblick nichts ausdrücken.* Letter from Friedl Dicker-Brandeis, Hronov, to Hilde Kothny, 1940.

4. Friedl Dicker studied there from 1912 to 1914.

5. Franz Čížek (1865 Litoměřice –1946 Vienna).

6. Johannes Itten (1888 Süderlinden–1967 Zürich), painter, teacher at the Bauhaus 1919 to 1923.

7. Walter Gropius (1883 Berlin–1969 Boston), architect, director of the Bauhaus from 1919 to 1928.

8. *Annylein, geliebtes, mich packt eine grosse Angst vor dem Alleinsein, vor dem ganzen Allein. Gebe mir Gott, dass ich diese Stadium überwinde.* Letter to Anny Wottitz, undated—probably 1921.

9. Georg Muche (1895 Querfurt/Saxony–1987 Lindau/ Bodensee), was designated "Meister der Form" in the 1920 Bauhaus textile workshop; he later taught at Itten's private school in Berlin (1927–1931).

10. Lyonel Feininger (1871 New York–1956 New York) taught at the Bauhaus during the entire time of the school's existence and was one of its more prominent artists.

11. Oskar Schlemmer (1888 Stuttgart–1943 Baden-Baden) taught at the Bauhaus from 1920 to 1929. In the beginning his position was as "Formmeister" in the sculpture atelier; he took over the "Bauhaus-Bühne" in 1923, continuing in this position even after the school was relocated to Dessau.

12. Adolf Hölzel (1853 Olomouc, Moravia–1934 Stuttgart).

13. See Johannes Itten, "Analysen alter Meister," in *Utopia: Dokumente der Wirklichkeit*, ed. Bruno Adler (Weimar: Utopia Verlag, 1921; reprint Munich, 1980).

14. See p. 91.

15. See p. 88.

16. Dicker worked together with Franz Singer on the design of the Heriots' villa.

17. Hans Hildebrandt (1878–1957) on Dicker's St. Anne Selbdritt: *"Von ganz anderer Art ist das eingliedernde Bildwek 'Anna Selbdritt' Friedl Dickers, die zu den vielseitigsten und originalsten Frauenbegabungen der Gegenwart zählt. Denkbar nur in dem Bau moderner Prägung, passt es sich diesem allerdings so organisch ein, dass es als Teil der Architektur erscheint. Die verwendeten Stoffe, Nickel, schwarzes Eisen, Messing, Glas, weisser und roter Lack, unterscheiden sich ebenso sehr von den herkömmlichen, wie die Gestaltung menschllicher Körper aus Röhren, Kugeln und Kegeln abweicht von der bislang üblichen. Die Unbedenk lichkeit der weiblichen Natur, die, einmal radikalisiert, alle Hemmungen beiseite wirft, lebt sich in diesem Bildwerk aus, das mehr ist als ein lebt-interestantes Experiment."* Hans Hildebrandt, *Die Frau aus Künstlerin* (Berlin, 1928).

18. Charcoal drawing, 1931; Pařík, cat. no. 25.

19. Charcoal drawing, 1931; Elena Makarova, *Friedl Dicker-Brandeis: Ein Leben für Kunst und Lehre* (Vienna, 1999), 105.

20. Oil on canvas, 1937–38; Makarova, 124.

21. Paul Klee (1879 Münchenbuchsee near Bern–1940 Muralto-Locarno) taught at State Bauhaus between 1920 and 1931; he conducted the glass painting atelier, although his influence on the work of the textile atelier was more important.

22. For a detailed analysis of the impact of children's drawings on modern painting, especially on the works fo individual representatives of classical modernism, see Jonathan Fineberg, *The Innocent Eye* (Princeton, 1997).

23. Ibid.

24. In 1923 Friedl Dicker and Franz Singer collaborated on the stage and costume design for Ibsen's *John Gabriel Borkman* (April), and Shakespeare's *The Merchant of Venice* (September), and at the end of the year Musil's comedy *Vinzenz oder die Freundin bedeutender Männer*.

25. "Kunstschau" (Berlin, 1927) and the exhibition "Modernes Design" (Vienna, 1929).

Friedl Dicker-Brandeis
*View from a Window
(in Františkovy Lázne)*
Pastel on paper
55 x 41 cm
c. 1936/37
The Jewish Museum, Prague
#176.359

Friedl Dicker-Brandeis
View from a Window
(Friedl's Room in L410, Terezín)
Pastel on paper
49 x 32 cm
c. 1944
Simon Wiesenthal Museum of Tolerance,
Los Angeles

26. *Das Bild von Heimat, von Boden ist nur ein Bild, und wir sind keine Götzenanbeter, wenn wir entwürzelt sind.* Letter from Friedl Dicker-Brandeis, Prague, to Anny Wottitz (Moller), undated.

27. A drawing with the noticeable features of a self-portrait, it was also called *Self-portrait in a Car*, pastel, 1940; Markarova, 131.

28. *Interrogation I*, oil on plywood, 1934/35; *Interrogation II*, oil on canvas, 1934/15; Makarova, 110–11.

29. *Self-portrait I*, charcoal, 1919–23, see p. 104; *Self-portrait II*, charcoal, 1919–23, hitherto unpublished, see p. 94.

30. *View of the Vltava under Vyšehrad*, oil on canvas, ca. 1936; Makarova, 109 and *View of the Vltava Embankment by the Railroad Bridge*, oil on canvas, ca. 1936; Makarova, 114.

31. *View to a Narrow Street in Prague-Nusle*, oil on canvas, ca. 1936; Makarova, 108.

32. These measures entered into force on March 15, 1939 with the occupation of Bohemia and Moravia by German forces and the proclamation of the Protectorate of Bohemia and Moravia.

33. *Still Life with Vases, Flowers, and Pomegranates*, oil on canvas, 1936; Makarova, 122 and *Small and Large Griffin*, oil on canvas, 1936, Makarova, 122.

34. *Self-portrait in a Car* as well as the playful *Still Life with Toys* (pastel, 1938–1940; Pařík, cat. no. 29), which refers to a children's drawing, and the portraits of her friends in Hronov and flower still lifes, which are modeled with a painter's sense for the distribution of color fields.

35. Oil on canvas, 1936; Makarova, 123.

36. Oil on canvas, 1940–42; Makarova, 152–53.

37. See pp. 98 and 101–02.

Translations from German into English by Kevin Blahu

BIBLIOGRAPHY

Bothe, Rolf von, Peter Hahn, and Hans Christoph von Tavel, eds. *Das frühe Bauhaus und Johannes Itten*. Katalogbuch anläßlich des 75. Gründungsjubiläums des Staatlichen Bauhauses in Weimar. Ostfildern-Ruit: G. Hatje, 1994.

Brugger, Ingried, ed. *Jahrhundert der Frauen. Vom Impressionismus zur Gegenwart. Osterreich 1870 bis heute*. Exhibition catalog, Oct. 1999–Jan. 2000. Wien: Kunstforum, 1999.

Fineberg, Jonathan. *The Innocent Eye: Children's Art and the Modern Artist*. Princeton: Princeton University Press, 1997.

Hildebrandt, Hans. *Die Frau als Künstlerin*. Berlin: Moose, 1928.

Makarova, Elena. *From Bauhaus to Terezín: Friedl Dicker-Brandeis and Her Pupils*. Exhibition catalog, Summer 1990. Jerusalem: Yad Vashem, 1990.

Makarova, Elena. *Friedl Dicker-Brandeis. Ein Leben für Kunst und Lehre. Wien Weimar Prag Hronov Theresienstadt Auschwitz*. Exhibition catalog, Simon Wiesenthal Center, Palais Harrach, Nov. 1999–Jan. 2000. Vienna: Christian Brandstätter Verlag, 1999.

Pařík, Arno. *Friedl Dicker-Brandeis 1898–1944*. Exhibition to Commemorate the 90th Anniversary of her Birthday, Exhibition catalog. Prague: State Jewish Museum in Prague, 1988.

Wingler, Hans M. *Das Bauhaus. 1919-1933 Weimar Dessau Berlin und die Nachfolge in Chicago seit 1937*, rev. 3rd ed. Schauberg: Verlag Gebr. Rash & Co. and M. DuMont, 1975.

Doris Kindler
Watercolor on paper
Born April 18, 1932
Deported to Terezín
December 17, 1941
Deported to Auschwitz
May 18, 1944
Perished
*The Jewish Museum, Prague
#131.816*

**It is only here that I learned
how complex transformations are
and that it is finally the endurance,
the unlimited perseverance,
which counts.**

From Friedl's Birthday Wish
to Willy Groag, Terezín, 1943

as cited in Elena Makarova,
*From Bauhaus to Terezín:
Friedl Dicker-Brandeis and Her Pupils*
(Jerusalem, 1990), 37

Friedl Dicker
Self-portrait I
Charcoal on paper
51.8 x 41.8 cm
c. 1920
The Jewish Museum, Prague
#176.278

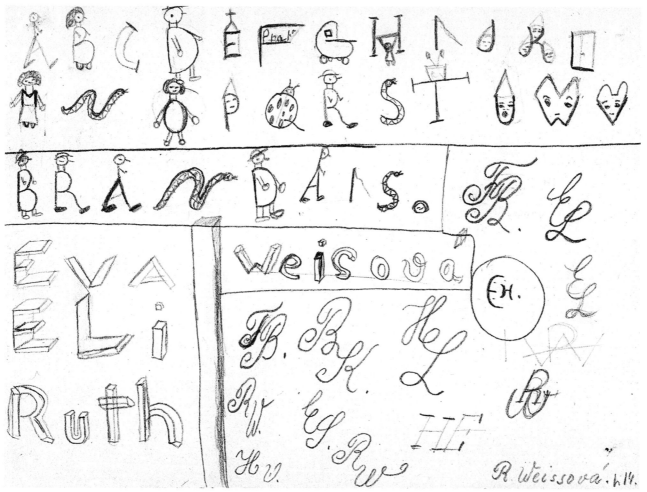

Ruth Weiss
Pencil on paper
20.9 x 27.6 cm
Born March 16, 1931
Deported to Terezín
November 20, 1942
Deported to Auschwitz
May 18, 1944
Perished

The Jewish Museum, Prague
#130.507

Ivo Hanuš Kauders
Pencil on paper
Born December 17, 1929
Deported to Terezín
May 12, 1942
Deported to Auschwitz
June 10, 1944
Perished
The Jewish Museum, Prague
#131.968r

Johannes Itten
Lithograph with a Figural Theme, 1919
Courtesy of the Estate of Johannes Itten

SUSAN LESHNOFF

Within the context of art education, the program of instruction at the Bauhaus in Germany between the years 1919 and 1933 commonly brings to mind architecture, the industrialization of crafts and the design education curriculum. Although most design foundation courses in art schools and colleges today are indebted to Bauhaus art education—and particularly to the preliminary course taught there by Johannes Itten from 1919 until 1923—the non-objective exercises concentrating on specific art elements, design principles, and variety of materials derived from Bauhaus instruction were not originally conceived as a purely experimental application of art theory.

Johannes Itten, along with the majority of other artists appointed by Walter Gropius, viewed art as an expression of one's spiritual resources. It was in this context that Friedl Dicker immersed herself for four years of artistic training.

Prior to studying at the Bauhaus, Dicker studied art under Franz Čížek who taught at the Vienna School of Applied Arts. Čížek was known for his innovative children's art classes where he encouraged children to present in visual form their personal reactions to experiences in their lives. Instead of having young students complete traditional copy exercises in art, Čížek encouraged children to develop self-expressive, creative, and often childlike imagery.[1]

When analyzing the artwork produced by children at Terezín, one can clearly perceive the influence of Čížek's art educational philosophy as well as Itten's experiments with design elements and materials. Friedl Dicker's way of inspiring artistic production among the children at Terezín owes much to her years in the company of Itten and the spiritual atmosphere that pervaded the early years of the Bauhaus.

Friedl Dicker began her studies with Johannes Itten (1888–1967) in Vienna in 1916, three years before he was invited to teach at the Bauhaus in Weimar Germany, then under the direction of Walter Gropius. From Itten's writings about the preliminary course that he taught at the Bauhaus, he made a clear connection between the activity of the soul and the recovery of intuitive creativity as the basis for teaching art. He and other artists appointed at the Bauhaus—Vasily Kandinsky, Georg Muche, Paul Klee, Oskar Schlemmer, Lothar Schreyer, and Lyonel Feininger[2]— shared the belief that being in touch with one's spiritual resources triggers creativity.

From the beginning days at the Bauhaus, Gropius selected artists as instructors who shared his utopian view of that art education could help transform the moral and ethical climate of

Johannes Itten in 1921
Bauhaus-Archiv, Berlin #8975

society. These artists were primarily connected with the abstract, transcendental branch of the Expressionist movement,[3] a movement associated with mysticism, universalism and the "cosmic."[4] After World War I, Expressionism, having departed from traditional academic art, was perceived as the visual symbol associated with utopian socialism.[5]

Itten, who was acquainted with Expressionist artists before his arrival at the Bauhaus, experimented with abstraction to evoke a sense of illusory movement which he associated with the essential vitality of life.[6] He organized a Basic Course that was compulsory for all new students during the early years of the Bauhaus. Successful completion of the six month course allowed students to continue study at the Bauhaus in a selected workshop. The purpose of the preliminary course was, according to Itten, "to liberate the creative forces and thereby the artistic talents of the students."[7]

Believing that imagination and artistic method both had to be strengthened, Itten developed a teaching method that trained the mind, the body, the senses, and the emotions. Itten sought to have each student make contact with the core of his natural creative center. He believed that "experiencing is a faculty of the mind and spirit,"[8] and aimed at having each student experience the essence of the object/subject before him and then recreate it artistically:

For a genuine feeling to be expressed in a line or area, it must, first of all, vibrate in the creative artist himself. Arm, hand, fingers, last but not least the whole body should be infused with this feeling. Such a devotion to the work requires both ability to concentrate and a relaxed frame of mind . . . Superficially fixed seeing, fluctuating thinking, and deliberate acting must give way to inner vision.[9]

In order to achieve this goal, Itten began each preliminary class with breathing and concentration exercises "to establish the intellectual and physical readiness which make intensive work possible."[10] He taught the students to relax the body in three ways: by moving the arms and legs and "bending and turning the body with special regard to the mobility of the spinal column;" by keeping the body perfectly still, "relaxing one part after another by thought concentration;" and by utilizing sound vibration for "balancing, relaxing, and harmonizing the body."[11] In addition, he instructed his students to breathe quietly and deeply, combining this process with training in thought concentration. Paul Klee, after visiting a session of Itten's Basic Course, wrote in a letter to his wife: "What is intended seems to be a kind of body massage to train the body machine to function sensitively."[12]

Itten was a student of Mazdeism. A derivative of ancient Zoroastrianism, Mazdeism (from the name of the good principle Ahura-Mazda) preached that through the proper use of the body the human being could direct all emotional, physical, and intellectual powers into a harmonious balance.[13] Fasting, purges, meditation, vegetarianism, and breathing exercises were Mazdean practices that were believed to restore inner peace—and which Itten believed were needed to free one's creative power. Regarding this philosophy, Itten wrote that "every pupil is burdened with a mass of learned materials which he must throw off in order to arrive at experience and his own awareness."[14]

So influential was Itten's teaching philosophy that for about two years the Bauhaus kitchen adopted a Mazdean menu. Regarding the diet, Oskar Schlemmer wrote to Otto Meyer-Amden on July 14, 1921, that Itten "regards it as the only way to the creation of the new man and he believes that a reform of habits of thought or feeling is essential before any progress in artistic creativity can be made."[15]

Georg Muche (1895–1987) was hired to teach at the Bauhaus in 1920 and to aid Itten in teaching the foundation course. He, along with Itten, began to convert students to Mazdeism at the Bauhaus.[16] Regarding his role as an art educator and an artist, Muche stated, "We sought the mysteries of creation, the hidden invisible side of nature and met a crystal clear vision of the boundlessness of our imagination."[17]

Itten was also assisted by Gertrude Grunow (1870–1944), a music teacher, who was hired at Itten's request because of their common thinking. She remained at the Bauhaus from 1919 until 1923, and like Itten, believed that inner harmony was a "necessary prerequisite for human creativity."[18] Grunow held classes in harmonization in which she imparted the belief that each person can rediscover a universal equilibrium based upon color, music, perception and form—and can access this equilibrium through physical and mental exercises.[19] The rewritten Bauhaus constitution of 1922 contained an amendment regarding Grunow's harmonization classes:

Eva Schur
Pastel on paper
Born June 2, 1935
Deported to Terezín
December 9, 1942
Deported to Auschwitz
May 15, 1944
Perished
The Jewish Museum, Prague
#133.234

110

"During the entire duration of study, practical harmonization classes on the common basis of sound, color and form will be taught with the aim of creating a balance between the physical and mental properties of the individual."[20] Itten resigned from the Bauhaus in 1923 primarily because he opposed the commercial contracts that the Bauhaus was seeking at that time. Muche and Grunow also left that year, along with many of his students, including Friedl Dicker.

It is known through a written lecture that Dicker delivered entitled, "On Children's Art," to the teachers at Home L417 at Terezín that her teaching strategy and philosophy drew from Itten's Basic Course. In that lecture she explained that "rhythmic exercise must make both the artist himself and his hand inspired

and supple. . . Exercises allow children to break from the routine in both vision and thought. . . ."[21] Thus, for example, the children visualized in line the rhythms and changes in voice quality that Dicker intoned.

Erna Furman, one of Dicker's older students at Terezín, wrote in a letter (1989) that during those art classes "we did a lot of 'freeing up' exercises, drawing circles and squiggles and letting our hands go, as well as using scissors freely."[22] Furman also wrote about her teacher: "At the time she conveyed peace, containment and a special way of looking. . . we never talked about personal matters. And that was good too because it kept out personal tragedies apart and allowed our drawing to be the most important thing."[23] Friedl understood that, if totally engrossing, the act of drawing and such 'freeing up' exercises, as well as utilizing one's full concentration had the power to lift and liberate students from daily concerns and fears. It would appear that Dicker's teaching techniques and philosophy were significantly influenced by the pervasive atmosphere created by Itten at the Bauhaus during her four years there.

Both Itten and Dicker aimed at liberating the creative forces in the individual. However, other instructors known as Masters of Form, who taught at the Bauhaus during Dicker's

Marianna Rosenzweig
(Room 28)
Charcoal
Born November 7, 1929
Deported to Terezín
September 30, 1942
Deported to Auschwitz
May 15, 1944
Survived
The Jewish Museum, Prague
#131.505v

residence, also taught and wrote about the absolute necessity of being in touch with one's spiritual center as a prerequisite for genuine creative expression. As one of the leading schools for the training of craftspeople in the early twentieth century, the Bauhaus gained much of its reputation by the appointment of well-known artists to its faculty. These artists, in an effort to inspire greater creativity from their students, relied on their spiritual resources for their own exemplary artistic production and included this spiritual dimension in their pedagogy. Essentially, they believed that the source for self-expression in art was the spiritual center of the individual.

Vasily Kandinsky (1866–1944), who joined the faculty in 1922, had written *Concerning the Spiritual in Art* eleven years earlier. In that volume he wrote that the artist "must search deeply into his soul, develop and tend it, so that his art has something to clothe and does not remain a glove without a hand."[24] Kandinsky's spiritual concerns partly centered on releasing the inner need of artists to realize a nonmaterial experience as an artistic form:

The spiritual life, to which art belongs, and of which she [art] is one of the mightiest elements, is a complicated but definite and easily definable movement forwards and upwards. This movement is the movement of experience. It may take

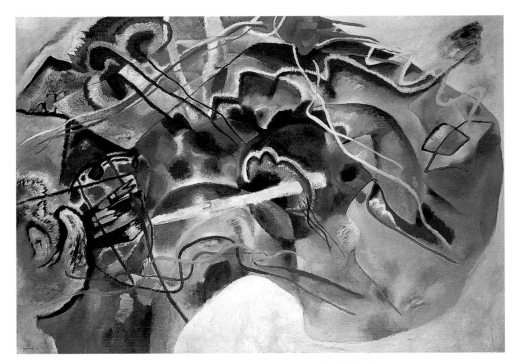

Vasily Kandinsky
Painting with White Border
May 1913
Oil on canvas
55 ¼" x 78 ⅞"
*Solomon R. Guggenheim Museum,
New York*

Robert Perl
Pastel on paper
Born June 6, 1932
Deported to Terezín
March 6, 1943
Deported to Auschwitz
October 4, 1944
Perished
The Jewish Museum, Prague
#133.249

different forms, but it holds at bottom to the same inner thought and experience.[25]

Kandinsky stated that in painting, artists are seeking "a road" leading inward to the spirit, that the spirit must be exercised for creative expression and that "the starting point for the exercise of the spirit. . . is the study of color."[26] Kandinsky believed that artistic expression was the outcome of working in unison with one's spirit. In 1914, Kandinsky prepared a lecture in Cologne in which he stated that "the genesis of the work [of art] is cosmic in character. The originator of the work is thus the spirit. The work exists abstractly even before it has been embodied, before it has become accessible to human senses."[27] Clearly Kandinsky's attitude toward artistic creation necessitated direct contact with one's spirit and its release into artistic form.

While at the Bauhaus, Friedl Dicker participated in workshops run by Paul Klee, Georg Muche, Oskar Schlemmer and Lyonel Feininger.[28] Paul Klee (1879–1940), who remained as a Master at the Bauhaus from 1921 until 1931, also taught about the "inner necessity" from which art is made.[29] He viewed man as part of nature: "The artist is a man, himself nature, and a part of nature within natural space."[30] Klee stated to a teacher of a group of art students:

As their talent develops guide your pupils toward Nature—into Nature. Make them experience how a bud is born, how a tree grows, how a butterfly unfolds, so that they may become just as resourceful, flexible, and determined as great Nature.[31]

Klee also viewed the artist within a cosmic framework, stating in 1923 that the artist "is a creature in the earth and a creature within the whole, that is, a creature on a star among stars."[32] He saw creation as a unifying act that derived from a primeval power. The act of creation, for Klee, was an ongoing process that dated back historically and projected into the future.

Klee perceived the making of art as a process that paralleled the process of cosmic creation. For clarification, he drew a comparison between the child who imitates adults and the artists who in play "imitate the forces which created and create the world."[33] Indeed, Klee stated that art "may help man to take off his cover and for a few moments imagine himself to be God."[34]

Klee felt that if the artist could adopt this way of viewing existence—by tracing natural form back to its creative source—and, at the same time view nature within the ongoing process of creation, the energy of what Klee called "Genesis eternal"[35] might well fuel the artist's own creative powers in a parallel manner. He said, "Such mobility of thought in the process of natural creation is good training for creative work. It has the power to move the artist fundamentally. . . ."[36]

According to Klee, the artist, by focusing on the primeval power can "more readily. . . extend his view from the present to the past, the more deeply he is impressed by the one essential image of creation, itself, as Genesis, rather than by the image of nature, the finished product."[37]

Klee associated abstract artistic expression and the intuitive process with a realm beyond the visible world. In his essay, "Ways of Nature Study," Klee viewed the artist as a creator who with a maturing philosophical outlook about being part of nature, could achieve "a completely free representation of abstract shapes beyond the consciously schematic approach."[38] According to Klee, the naturalness of this approach would lead to "the creation of works that are the image of God's work."[39]

For Klee, abstract art was derived from a more spiritual source. For him, the real truth remained invisible, and the true work of the artist was to make visible that which underlies or lies beyond material reality. In a 1913 entry in his diary, Klee discussed the quality of line "as absolute spirituality without analytical accessories."[40]

Walter Gropius and Adolf Meyer
Umbau Stadttheater Jena, 1921–22
Foyer mit Kasse
Bauhaus Archiv, Berlin

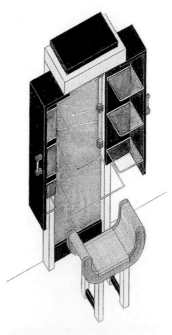

Friedl Dicker
Stack of Drawers for Sheet Music,
Apartment of Alice Moller
Ink, pencil, and colored
pencil on paper, 1928
Collection of Georg Schrom

Oskar Schlemmer (1888–1943), who taught at the Bauhaus from 1921 until 1929. stated that "total self-absorption" led to a sense of oneness with God, the universe, nature and existence from the time of Creation:

> Like the mystics, today's artists hope to pass through total self-absorption to oneness with God and the Universe. Everything is part of nature, part of the fabric of the universe. The man of our times cannot shut out the richness of everyday experience, the fullness of the Creation and of history.[41]

Like Klee, Schlemmer perceived the artist within a cosmic framework and connected to God through the spirit. Schlemmer believed that artists strive to express an idea derived from the times or from inner subjectivity. However, it is the spirit that energizes the artistic process. He wrote in 1915: "I remain convinced that the idea is the source of form; the spirit guides the hand."[42]

Another dimension of the innovative Bauhaus program was that it included a theater workshop. Theater, itself, was viewed by Walter Gropius as an opportunity for transcendental experience. In 1922 Gropius wrote in a draft that was to be in a brochure on the Bauhaus Theater:

> In its very origins the stage arose from man's religious yearnings (Theater = seeing God). Its task is to make manifest a transcendental idea. Therefore, its impact on the soul of the spectator and hearer is dependent on its success in

translating the idea into the realms of perception (optical and auditory).[43]

In 1921 Gropius appointed Lothar Schreyer (1886–1966) to the Bauhaus faculty where he supervised Theater Workshop, a position he held until 1923. For a time Dicker attended this workshop and participated in Schreyer's play, "*Mondspiel*," "Moon Play."[44] Schreyer also contributed to the spiritual ideas permeating the Bauhaus during the early years of its existence. A highly religious personality, Schreyer clung to the tenets of Christianity in theater performance, in poetry, and in his expressionistic painting. Regarding his theatrical productions at the Bauhaus, Schreyer wrote: "Our theater workshop sought to serve the revelation of the hidden, spiritual world in the midst of the cosmic powers."[45]

Schreyer sought to achieve a common "mystical-cultic experience" between actors and audience. His plays had no dialogue, but rather sound effects differing in pitch, volume, timbre, and rhythm used in "shouts, wails, chants and incantations,"[46] His performers wore large geometrically-formed masks that entirely covered their bodies. In the introduction to one of his plays, Schreyer wrote that the actors for this play are not to be professional: "Anyone can act this play who can see himself, hear himself, stand outside himself, who follows the play without reservation and who lives in a community with the other players."[47] Of the audience he wrote: "Those who hear and see the scenario must know: The play can be seen and heard only in a circle of friends as a common experience, as a common act of devotion, as a common creation."[48]

What Schreyer hoped to achieve was a mystical experience shared by actors and audience alike, the play being used as a medium for spiritual transcendence. This goal was philosophically in line with Gropius's desire for theater's impact on the Bauhaus audience. Schreyer's religious mystery play, "Moon Play," was unpopular among students at Bauhaus and led to his resignation from the faculty in 1923. The attachment of spiritual values to a specified religious belief did not find much acceptance there.

Although Lyonel Feininger (1871–1956) was among the first three teachers appointed by Gropius to be a Master of Form at the Bauhaus, his interest in teaching was not so strong as his desire to paint privately in his studio.[49] Although he remained at the school until its closing in 1933, he taught very little and was permitted to stop teaching altogether in 1926.[50] According to Whitford,[51] it is not understood how Gropius viewed Feininger's contribution to Bauhaus teaching.

Friedl Dicker
*Portrait of a Man with a Moustache
(Walter Gropius?)*
Charcoal on paper
78 x 63 cm
The Jewish Museum, Prague
#176.280

116

Trude Hofmeister
Watercolor
Born November 11, 1930
Deported to Terezín
March 19, 1942
Deported to Auschwitz
October 23, 1944
Perished
The Jewish Museum, Prague
#133.536

Schlemmer wrote that the model Feininger offered the students was inspirational: " 'Though he [Feininger], to all appearance, scarcely participated in the teaching, his demeanor and his accomplishment served as a constant example. He spread the atmosphere of concentration and meditation which is essential to creative life.' "[52] In 1919 Feininger wrote in a letter to his wife: "I am concerned with the spiritual side of art."[53]

The only formal art training Friedl Dicker had were her four years at the Bauhaus. A lecture entitled "Children's Drawings," delivered to teachers at Terezín in 1943 shortly before her deportation to Auschwitz, outlined teaching principles in part drawn from what she learned at the Bauhaus:

> Drawing must free and make full use of such sources and energies as creativity and independence; it must awaken fantasy; it must strengthen the natural abilities of observation and appreciation of reality. . . In determining children's paths we. . . sever them from their own creative experience. They are torn from their own tasks. On this path the child loses first the individual means of expression appropriate to his life experience, then the experience itself. Mastery of prepared forms too soon leads to the enslaving of personality.[54]

With parallel thoughts on the significance of independent but authentic self-expression in art, Itten described the principal aim of the teacher in his book *Design and Form: the Basic Course at the Bauhaus and Later.*

It should be the principal aim of any teacher to promote the growth of genuine observation, genuine feeling, and genuine thinking. Empty superficial imitations should be removed like objectionable warts. Encouragement to return to the original creative condition liberates students from the constraints imposed on them by the facts they have absorbed merely from mechanical learning.[55]

Robert Welleminsk
Watercolor
Born July 7, 1931
Deported to Terezín
January 30, 1942
Deported to Auschwitz
May 15, 1944
Perished

The Jewish Museum, Prague
#133.446

Itten described authentically creative work by the individual as a genuine "formalization of a subject [for art]"—one that corresponded to the "creative artist's constitution and temperament."[56] He divided artistic personalities into three types: the material/impressive type who seeks to achieve realistic observation in drawings; the intellectual/constructive type who analyzes the structure of a subject and orders it geometrically in drawings; and the spiritual/expressive type "who allows himself to be guided by his intuition" in drawing.[57] In nature classes Itten asked students to interpret the same object from these three orientations—as realistic observation, as an intellectual/construction, and as a spiritual/expressive visual statement. In a fourth work, students were to find their own compromise among these orientations in line with their temperaments. In his own words, then, Itten linked the spiritual and the expressive together, as other Bauhaus Masters did who described genuine self-expressiveness as emanating from a spiritual center.

Friedl Dicker-Brandeis in her lecture "Children's Drawings," also stressed the importance of choosing one's own artistic path. According to her, through art production, fantasy, intellect and a "gift for observation" would develop in the child. Her belief was also that

Eva Schur
Pastel on paper
Born June 2, 1935
Deported to Terezín
December 9, 1942
Deported to Auschwitz
May 15, 1944
Perished

The Jewish Museum, Prague
#133.159

art production could have an impact on the development of personality. She stated that "through independent choice, discovery and exploration of form, the child becomes stable and sincere."[58] She also stated that "all of this ensures the road to beauty."[59]

Friedl Dicker-Brandeis wrote these words in the midst of horrific destruction of human life at Terezín. The assurance of a "road to beauty," if not a physical reality, was a spiritual possibility through art production for herself as well as for her young students. As Raya Englenderová, a Terezín student survivor, wrote, "Mrs. Brandeis. . . managed for some hours every week — to create a fairy world for us in Terezín. . . a world that made us forget all the surrounding hardships. . . . "[60]

In his book, *Concerning the Spiritual in Art*, Kandinsky wrote about a road to the spirit[61] through artistic exercises. The spiritual path that Dicker herself followed at the Bauhaus might very well have been the "road to beauty" she hoped her students at Terezín would not only encounter, but also travel, in the process of making art. This was certainly a path that transcended time and place.

NOTES

1. Čížek is credited with pioneering efforts to allow his students personal self-expression in art. To what extent childlike freedom of expression was allowable in his classes is debatable. Regarding this controversy see "Franz Čížek and the Elusiveness of Historical Knowledge," in P. Smith, *The History of American Art Education: Learning About Art in American Schools* (Westport Conn 1996) 59–78.

2. H. Wingler, ed., *The Bauhaus,* trans. W. Jabs and B. Gilbert, (Cambridge, 1969), 253. According to Wingler, it was primarily due to Itten's influence that Gropius appointed Muche, Schlemmer, Klee, and Kandinsky.

3. R. W. Long, "Expressionism, Abstraction, and the Search for Utopia in Germany," in *The Spiritual in Art: Abstract Painting 1890–1985,* ed., E. Weisberger, (New York, 1986), 208.

4. Ibid., 201 and 216. In fn. 1, Long refers to two texts for a discussion of the early use of the term Expressionism in Germany: Marie Werenskiold, *The Concept of Expressionism: Origin and Metamorphoses,* trans. Ronald Walford, (Oslo, 1984); and Victor Miesel, "The Term Expressionism in the Visual Arts (1911–1920)," in *The Uses of History,* ed. Hayden White, (Detroit, 1968), 135–51.

5. Long, 201.

6. Ibid., 211.

7. J. Itten, *Design and Form* (New York, 1975), 7. (Original work published in 1926)

8. Wingler, 49.

9. Itten, 110.

10. Ibid., 9.

11. Ibid.

12. Ibid., 12.

13. M. Fransciscono, *Walter Gropius and the Creation of the Bauhaus in Weimer: The Ideals and Artistic Theories of its Founding Years* (Urbana, 1971), 194.

14. Ibid., 191.

Hanna Wertheimer (Room 28)
Collage
Born December 12, 1929
Deported to Terezín
March 3, 1942
Deported to Auschwitz
May 18, 1944
Survived
The Jewish Museum, Prague
#131.686

15. E. Roters, *Painters of the Bauhaus*, trans. A. Cooper, (New York, 1969), 49.

16. M. Droste, *Bauhaus 1919–1933*, trans. K. Williams, (Berlin, 1993), 32.

17. F. Whitford, *Bauhaus* (London, 1984), 92.

18. Droste, 33.

19. Ibid.

20. Ibid.

21. E. Makarova, *From Bauhaus to Terezín* (Jerusalem, 1990), 6; idem, *Friedl Dicker-Brandeis: Ein Leben für Kunst und Lehre* (Vienna, 2000).

22. Makarova, *From Bauhaus to Terezín*, 38.

23. Ibid.

24. V. Kandinsky, *Concerning the Spiritual in Art*, trans. M. Sadler (New York, 1977), 54. (Original work published in 1911)

25. Ibid., 4.

26. Ibid., 35–36.

27. W. Grohmann, *Kandinsky: Life and Work*, trans. N. Guterman (New York, 1958), 92.

28. Makarova, *Friedl Dicker-Brandeis*, 16.

29. Whitford, 98.

30. Wingler, 73.

31. R. Verdi, *Klee and Nature* (New York, 1984), 26.

32. Wingler, 73.

33. B. Tower, *Klee and Kandinsky in Munich and at the Bauhaus*, (Ann Arbor, 1981), 130.

34. Ibid., 131.

35. P. Klee, *Paul Klee on Modern Art*, trans. P. Findlay (London, 1984), 45.

36. Ibid., 47.

37. Ibid., 45.

38. Wingler, 73.

39. Ibid.

40. Tower, 110.

41. T. Schlemmer, ed., *The Letters and Diaries of Oskar Schlemmer*, trans. K. Winston (Middletown, 1972), 53.

42. Ibid., 29.

43. W. Gropius, *The Theater of the Bauhaus*, trans. A. Wensinger (Middletown, 1961), 81.

44. Makarova, *Friedl Dicker-Brandeis*, 18.

45. H. Dearstyne, *Inside the Bauhaus*, ed. Spaeth (New York, 1986), 173.

46. Forgacs, ed., *The Bauhaus Idea and Bauhaus Politics*, trans. J. Batki (Budapest, 1995), 59.

47. Roters, 67.

48. Ibid.

49. Ibid., 23.

50. Ibid., 28.

51. Whitford, 62.

52. Ibid.

53. Dearstyne, 106.

54. Makarova, *From Bauhaus to Terezín*, 32.

55. Itten, 132.

56. Ibid.

57. Ibid.

58. Makarova, *From Bauhaus to Terezín*, 32.

59. Ibid.

60. Ibid., 30.

61. Kandinsky, 35–36.

Hanuš Perl
Pencil on paper
Born January 8, 1932
Deported to Terezín
September 30, 1942
Deported to Auschwitz
October 12, 1944
Perished
The Jewish Museum, Prague
#133.433

Art, Music and Education as Strategies for Survival: Theresienstadt 1941–45

A CAROUSEL OF THEATRICAL PERFORMANCE IN THERESIENSTADT

If Terezín was not hell itself, like Auschwitz, it was the anteroom to hell. But culture was still possible, and for many this frenetical clinging to an almost hypertrophy of culture was the final assurance.

We are human beings and we remain human beings, they were saying in this way, despite everything! And if we must perish, the sacrifice must not have been made in vain. We must give it some meaning![1]

Norbert Frýd, "Culture in the Anteroom to Hell," *Terezin* (Prague: Council of Jewish Communities in the Czech Lands, 1965), 217

Bedřich Fritta
Ink on paper, n.d.
Courtesy of Thomas Fritta-Haas

REBECCA ROVIT

Inmates at Terezín (also known as Theresienstadt) used art in different ways to give some temporary meaning to their lives. While Friedl Dicker-Brandeis and her young pupils captured in their drawings their experiences of ghetto life in various ways, with a variety of media; imprisoned musicians, poets, theater artists and other amateur artists from Czechoslovakia, Germany, Austria, Holland, and Denmark—all Jews—relied on their art to provide themselves and their fellow inmates with a diversion, a "retreat," a "moral uplift" from the daily dreads and grueling workdays which most prisoners at Terezín endured.

Artists created theater within the ghetto administration's cultural department, known as *Freizeitgestaltung*, or "organized leisure time activity." The first director of this department, Rabbi Erich Weiner, reported on his role in the cultural program after it had officially begun in February 1942: "The leisure time activity and its tasks drew me completely under its spell. I saw progressive spiritual deterioration; I saw the brutalization of the ghetto inmates."[2] And looking back on his experiences in the ghetto, the stage director, Norbert Frýd, describes the inmates' hunger to participate in cultural programs, ". . . as a measure of the unbroken will to live."[3] Zdenka Fantlová, who performed in Frýd's 1943 production of *Esther*, has referred to the ghetto theater as "a support for the fighting

spirit."[4] Philipp Manes, the director of a lecture series and play readings in Theresienstadt, notes in his journal the unhappy effect of a month-long ban on all cultural activities in 1944. He writes, "It is hard to describe what this lack of activity meant for us in the evenings, how it depressed our state of mind."[5] Evident in these voices and those of others who performed or attended cultural events in Terezín is their direct association of theater art with spiritual uplift.

I will return to this idea as I survey some of the theatrical performances which occurred within an astounding range of concerts, cabarets, operas, and staged dramas at Theresienstadt from 1942 to 1945. The term "theater" implies an audience and the dramatic recitation of poetry; the performance of comic skits, songs, and dances, often commented on by an emcee as in cabaret; the production of libretti or playscripts—fully staged or simply read; and other entertainment like puppet shows which integrate theater with music and the applied arts. All of these types of performance took place in the ghetto. Initially clandestine, the performances were eventually tolerated, and then encouraged by the Council of Jewish Elders. By 1944, the SS Command actively supported and exploited the cultural programs.

Norbert Frýd

Born 1913, Prague
Deported to Terezín
August 7, 1943
Deported to Auschwitz
September 28, 1944
Survived
Terezín Memorial #387

Zdenka Fantlová

Born 1922
Deported to Terezín
January 1942
Deported to Auschwitz
October 16, 1944
Liberated from Bergen-Belsen
April 15, 1945
Survived
Photograph by Stephen M. Barth

Unknown Photographer
Still from the Nazi propaganda film,
*Theresienstadt: A Documentary Film from
the Jewish Settlement Area,* 1944
Terezín Memorial #A1893

Two unidentified men performing
on a temporary stage in a courtyard.

124

The performers included professionals and amateurs, most of whom volunteered their services to the cultural department. They chose to create theater, even though their performances usually began after a grueling eight-hour work day and rehearsals often took place after the performances were over.[6] Why did these performers sacrifice the little leisure time that they had for art's sake? And what kinds of performances did they enact? After all, there was no great material profit at stake for the artists, although some of them were privileged to live in houses for the so-called "Prominents." And Rabbi Weiner eventually managed to negotiate extra rations of sugar and margarine for those artists who worked overtime.[7] Theater at Terezín was in some sense a continuation of the theatrical traditions of the Prague avant-garde and the pre-war Viennese and Berlin cabaret; and we should expect the Czech theater performances to differ from the German-language theater. As I consider such questions, I will mainly focus on the cabaret to illustrate how theatrical performance may have enabled the inmates to retain some glint of hope in a desperately hopeless situation.

It should be emphasized that one can only suggest the breadth of creativity that was evident in Terezín. We simply do not have a complete record. Many of the performers and spectators did not survive to share their memories. Nor can we fully know the effect of the performances on the actors and their audience. We need to be aware of the different perspectives which shape the process of recreating theater performance at Terezín: there are uninterpreted documents; there are survivors who recall their experience of a documented event; and there are those of us who remain observers as students and scholars, our life experiences radically distancing us from these events. These perspectives may often contradict one another.

It is also vital to recognize that of all of the arts, theater art is the most ephemeral. The fleeting quality of theater is even more transient if performed in a ghetto like Theresienstadt. Under normal circumstances, one often has the performance text to read if that text has been written down, and not improvised, and if the text still exists. Yet, because a performance takes place and ends in real time, only those present can know about the performance event as it actually was. We must rely on those who were there to tell us about it. Thus it is obviously extraordinarily difficult to recreate a performance, especially one that took place in a ghetto where performers and spectators were targeted for deportation and extermination.

Given such obstacles, finding remnants of theatrical performance from Terezín has been surprisingly possible. This is in part because the Council of the Jewish Elders tolerated cultural activities in the ghetto. At first, they permitted the cultural department, but did not want the activities to be openly practiced. It was unclear how the Nazis would respond. The Jewish-run administration eventually issued official reports on the theatrical programs. And Weiner highlights the problems and achievements of the leisure-time activities as they developed. He tells us about the early dilemma of organizing cultural activities within the individual barracks. He describes the difficulty of acquiring "passage permits" for "guest performances" by men in the women's barracks, for example, when men and women's theatrical events were segregated. Weiner also announces the problem of finding vacant spaces for performances while transports were bringing thousands of new

Bedřich Fritta
Ink on paper, n.d.
Courtesy of Thomas Fritta-Haas

126

inmates into overcrowded barracks at the same time as the number of artistic groups in the ghetto expanded.

Other sources reveal different issues: during the ghetto's "beautification" in 1944, the Nazis deliberately exploited the arts programs. This was during the months when Commandant Karl Rahm stage-managed a physical transformation of Terezín for the benefit of international visitors, culminating in a coerced propaganda film, made by the imprisoned director and cabaret star, Kurt Gerron. Unfortunately, some of the existing documentation of the theatrical performances, like scenes from the children's opera, *Brundibár*, in the bogus film, *Theresienstadt: A Documentary Film from the Jewish Settlement Area,* also subsequently known as *The Führer gives a Town to the Jews*, greatly distorts the reality and significance of ghetto productions. To counter such distortions of the *Freizeitgestaltung*, there are memoirs by artists who survived Terezín and who have written about their participation in the theater there.

Some of these witnesses refer to the first-class theater artists and musicians from major European capitals, who continued their artistic work at Terezín. For example, Fantlová has suggested the significance of this talented group in providing mentorship and even a night-time acting seminar for the young Czech artists who created a vibrant theater in the ghetto.[8]

Helga Weissová-Hosková
Opera in the Loft
Pencil on paper
1944

A cameraman is shown filming a concert for the use in the 1944 propaganda film, *"The Führer Gives a Town to the Jews."*

Fortunately, such memoirs put us in a better position to evaluate the high quality of art created by some of these artists like the composers, Viktor Ullmann, Hans Krása, and the poet, Petr Kien, who left behind musical scores and libretti from the *Emperor of Atlantis* (written in Terezín) and *Brundibár* (1943). Although incomplete, we also have texts of cabaret skits and song lyrics by Leo Strauss and Manfred Greiffenhagen, among others, and original music from the German-language cabarets. Detailed analyses of the cabaret by the inmate theater critic, Josef ("Pepík") Taussig, have literally been unearthed at Terezín. And scenic designs and costume sketches for theatrical productions by such designers as František Zelenka survived the ghetto, as have the journals of

František Zelenka
Stage design for Cabaret
"Karussell" directed by Kurt Gerron,
performed in the Hamburg barracks,
Theresienstadt, 1944

National Museum
Theater History Department, Prague
#6752/52

Born September 13, 1905
Deported to Terezín
November 30, 1942
Deported to Auschwitz
October 16, 1944
Perished
Terezín Memorial #A9/99
Schächter was deported to
Auschwitz immediately after a
performance of Verdi's *Requiem*.

Philipp Manes.[9] These priceless materials are testaments to the leisure time activities at Theresienstadt.

To fully understand these activities, consider the three major administrative developments in the ghetto which directly affected the arts program as it evolved: the establishment of the "leisure time activity" early in 1942, the expansion of the ghetto later that fall, and the "beautification" phase of Theresienstadt.[10] Before the cultural department existed, theatrical performances were initially clandestine. Musical instruments were forbidden, for example, and loud applause was silenced. These so-called "fellowship evenings," were organized by the Czech professionals and privileged workers who had arrived with the two construction commando transports in late 1941. One of these men, Karel Švenk, soon developed these variety evenings into semi-legal cabaret evenings. His first satirical cabaret revue, *The Lost Food Card*, took place in the "potato peeling room" of the men's Sudeten barracks in 1942. Other performances took place in makeshift attic spaces. Jana Šedová (formerly known as Trude Popper) recalls the performances she initiated for women after hearing about Švenk's revue, "We played without costumes or stage so that no traces of our secret activities might be left behind."[11]

After the cultural department was established, and all non-Jews were evacuated from the ghetto, men and women were permitted to perform together and attend theater evenings. Additional rooms were made available to artists. These included a barracks' carpentry shop; the sleeping quarters of the Cavalier barracks, the potato peeling room (if it was available), and attic spaces. Later, in warm weather, courtyards were used for outdoor performances. As Theresienstadt expanded to meet the demands of new transports, afternoon variety shows were presented to boost the morale of newcomers. For these performances, new theater spaces had to be found. The Magdeburg barracks soon had a main stage, while provisional platforms were constructed in several attics. By spring 1944, once the "beautification" project was underway, Commandant Rahm had a new stage constructed in the Hamburg barracks for Kurt Gerron. And large-scale music productions took place in the refurbished Sokol gymnasium where visitors from the International Red Cross watched the reprise of *Brundibár* later that summer.

In spite of Nazi attempts to use the artists for propaganda purposes, many of those who were exploited insist that they had achieved something positive through their theater art. Those who engaged in the cultural programs dedicated themselves to their art almost in defiance of the horrific circumstances of their imprisonment. Yet Šedová has said that the theatrical performances ought not to be viewed as heroic. Rather, their significance was in fighting for what she calls "basic moral values." She writes, "The loss of human dignity could much more easily break the prisoners than starvation, forced labor, and maltreatment."[12] Herbert Exenberger remembers the positive effect of theater on him as a boy at Theresienstadt in 1943. Of performances by the Viennese cabarettist, Walter Lindenbaum, he writes: "with his lyricism, he tried, on the one hand, to lift his 'fellow-sufferers' out of the oppressing deprivation and despair; on the other hand, he documented this misery in his lyrics."[13]

What was this theater like that attempted to bring the spirit of normality temporarily to the ghetto? By late 1942, numerous artistic troupes flourished in Terezín. Among the dramas performed in Czech were plays and operas of different styles: Zdenek Jelinek's *Trap* was in the tradition of commedia dell'arte.[14] Anton Chekhov's one-acts, *The Bear* and *Courtship* were the first plays performed in costume. In 1943, Gustav Schorsch of Prague's National Theater directed Gogol's *The Marriage* with sets designed by Zelenka. In addition to Jean Cocteau's mono-opera, *The Human Voice*, performed by Vlasta Schönová (1942), E.F.

Burian's version of *Esther* (1943), and Molière's *Georges Dandin* (1943), there were Czech-language opera productions conducted by Rafael Schächter, including Smetana's *The Bartered Bride* (1942) and Mozart's *The Marriage of Figaro* (1943). Krása's *Brundibár* played more than fifty-five times at Terezín in 1943 and 1944. Meanwhile, the German-language theater centered around the cabaret, the opera, and play readings from classic literature. There were productions of Strauss's *Fledermaus* (1943), Verdi's *Rigoletto* (1943), Puccini's *Tosca* (1943), and Bizet's *Carmen* (1944).[15]

But cabaret was the most prevalent form of theater in Terezín. A cabaret requires only several performers and minimal materials and space. It was especially well-suited to ghetto life, because of the ease with which theatrical revues could be assembled, disassembled (if an SS guard might appear), and reassembled if a performer were ill or put on a transport.

Unknown Artist
Program cover
for Smetana's *The Bartered Bride*, 1942
*Terezín Memorial
#SOPT4295*

The attics provided the setting for the earliest cabaret performances. Frýd describes the barracks' gigantic two-story high roof supports made of wooden beams while hanging rags on rope made "grotesque" curtains.[16] Šedová's cabaret took place in such a setting. And the Viennese comedian, Bobby John, performed in the Dresden barracks attic on a gangway right in the middle of the inmates.[17] Fantlová performed with another cabaret group, led by Josef Lustig and Jiří Strauss, in the Magdeburg barracks; their satirical revues about Terezín life were in the tradition of Prague's pre-World War II "Liberated Theater."[18]

Among the German-language cabarets was that of Hans Hofer, who also directed one-acts by Arthur Schnitzler and Hugo Hofmannsthal on the attic stage of Q307. The music combo, the "Ghetto Swingers," appeared regularly in Hofer's cabaret during 1942.[19] Bobby John and Ernst Morgan soon organized their own cabarets, entertaining their audiences with jokes about unfaithful husbands, ugly wives, and domineering mother-in-laws. And while Walter Lindenbaum's nostalgic numbers about Vienna made the audiences cry, Walter Steiner's tribute to the past had an optimistic spirit, according to Josef Taussig.[20] Leo Strauss, the son of the Viennese composer Oscar Strauss, formed his own "Strauss Ensemble" with comic texts set to waltz music.

But Strauss also wrote cabaret numbers which may have helped the prisoners to tolerate the conditions in the ghetto, like his ironic sketch, *Theresienstadt Questions*, a dialogue between a veteran woman inmate and a new arrival from Vienna.[21] In other texts by Strauss or Manfred Greiffenhagen, the bitterness of the lyrics would often be melodiously rendered, the pretty music ironically contradicting the harshness of text.[22]

Strauss and Greiffenhagen wrote, perhaps, their most effective texts for Kurt Gerron who came to Terezín in late February 1944. By Spring, Gerron had assembled his own cabaret known as the "Karussell," with Zelenka designing the sets and costumes and jazz pianist, Martin Roman, of the "Ghetto Swingers," composing the music. Among Gerron's seasoned performers were the soprano, Anny Frey, and the tenor, Michel Gobets. The repertory included songs from Brecht and Weill's *Threepenny Opera*, which Gerron had made famous in 1928 with his interpretation of "Mack the Knife" and "The Canon Song." Gobets sang French chansons and Yiddish folksongs. And there were songs which were written in Theresienstadt."[23]

All of the cabarets, both Czech and German-language, employed ghetto humor. There were many songs and jokes about food or the lack of it. Cabarettists poked fun at the living conditions and how rumors spread in the ghetto. As preparations were underway for Terezín's "facelift" it was common to hear, "The beautification phase should last so long that we can say, 'We look beautiful.'" Or there was the joke about fleas: "All the fleas will be painted with phosphorous, so that the commission will think they're fireflies."[24] Hofer wrote parodies of songs from the *Fledermaus*, substituting the words with Theresienstadt slang. A recurrent theme in some of the revues was the future after Terezín. Ghetto slang and conventions were invariably used to comic advantage as skits depicted the clash of ghetto customs with supposedly "normal" ones.[25] One such scene portrayed a wife falling on her new maid's suitcase to scavenge through it.[26]

It appears that Czech poetry and theater at Terezín were more political and critical about society than the German-language theater.[27] Šedová has suggested that the German command may not have been fully aware that the Czech revues and plays had been performed in Czech. She recalls that while they reported each performance to the German authorities, they did so "often under a fictitious title."[28] Thus the Czechs may have risked satire because many of the Germans did not understand Czech. Many of the Czechs understood German and some of them, like Taussig and Frýd, attended the German-

Leo Haas
Cabaret in the Courtyard
Ink on paper, n.d
Terezín Memorial #SOPT 1884

language performances. According to Taussig, the "Germans" tended to rely on erotic double entendres, dancing girls, and a good dose of sentimentality.[29] One mixed "Czech-German Revue" from the women's Dresden barracks burlesqued the bureaucracy of the "housing" department; the Council of Elders; and featured numbers like the "Dance of the Cleaning Brigade" and the "Song of the Soldiers' Fight against Lice."[30]

But it was Karel Švenk who heralded a new brand of ghetto parody. The young Czechs—who were mostly in their twenties—sought new forms for their satiric presentation of ghetto concerns. Švenk's cabaret performances evidently went beyond a criticism of Terezín. His allegorical revue, *The Last Cyclist* (1943), was so provocative that the Jewish Council of Elders banned it before its premiere. The play's premise is an obvious parallel to the Third Reich: in a country under dictatorship, the cyclists become the scapegoats for all evil. Although the dictator tries to rid the country of all cyclists, one "last cyclist" prevails in the end. It is also true, however, that powerful German-language stage material was written in Terezín: Petr Kien's avant-garde *Puppets* was translated into Czech and performed by the Czechs. And his libretto to Ullmann's *The Emperor of Atlantis* was rehearsed in German under the direction of Karl Meinhard (1944). This opera was also banned by the Jewish Council of Elders after the final dress rehearsal for its allegorical parallels to a dictator, Emperor "Overall." Overall declares universal war, but Death goes on strike, so that no one can die. In the end, Death will only go back to work if the Emperor is the first to die.

Vitality prevailed under Philipp Manes's direction as well. Of thirty evenings a month allotted to Manes for lectures, eight to ten evenings were reserved for play readings.[31] Actors sat around a table and read such dramatic classics as the *Urfaust*, Goethe's *Faust I and II*, his *Iphigenia*, Hauptmann's *The Sunken Bell*, and Rostand's *Cyrano de Bergerac*. By August 1943, Lessing's play about religious tolerance, *Nathan the Wise*, had been performed fourteen times.[32] However, by September 1944, Manes had lost to transports those people whom he called, "the pillars of the ensemble," as well as many of the lecturers, who had been scheduled to speak in October.[33]

The organized play readings represent a poignant response to ghetto imprisonment. Great works of literature like *Faust* and *Nathan the Wise* transcend time with their universal themes of the search for knowledge and tolerance; man's temptation, downfall, and redemption. The poet, Gerty Spies, writes that Manes's dedication to intellectual pursuits at Theresienstadt was "our salvation."[34] Like Manes, Karel Švenk, Kurt Gerron, and his text writer, Manfred Greiffenhagen, tried to make theater respond to and transcend the situation in which they found themselves. Švenk used satire to kindle a kind of fighting spirit for the inmates. And Gerron, while being the Commandant's "official" cabaret performer, presented for his fellow inmates Greiffenhagen's incisive lyrics. In a kind of "doublespeak," Gerron commented on the predicament that he and his audience shared. In his cabaret's title song, "Carousel," Gerron himself sang Greiffenhagen's words of childhood hope and memory, calling attention to the reality of their imprisonment. The ride on the merry-go-round is a metaphor for a journey in "perpetual circles" with no destination. One cannot hop off in transit. Yet the merry-go-round keeps going day after day, moving without going anywhere: "Where we land at the end of our journey, we'll only find out when we stop."[35]

Kurt Gerron and Philipp Manes were deported to Auschwitz on October 28, 1944, where they both perished. Manfred Greiffenhagen was deported to Auschwitz on October 12, 1944 where he perished. Karel Švenk was deported to Auschwitz on October 1, 1944. He died in a German labor camp in 1945. I would like to believe that their efforts and those of their fellow artists at Terezín were not without meaning.

František Zelenka
Scenic flat for
Kurt Gerron's
Cabaret "Karussell"
National Museum,
Theater History Department
Prague #6753/52

NOTES

1. Norbert Frýd, "Culture in the Anteroom to Hell," in *Terezín* (Prague: Council of Jewish Communities in the Czech Lands, 1965), 207–17. The Czech theater director Frýd was deported to Terezín in August 1943. During his imprisonment, he staged a premiere adaptation of the folkplay *Esther*. This script had originally been prepared for the stage by E.F. Burian–the director of theater "D"–with whom Frýd had worked. Burian founded the theater in 1934 as "Theater D34" (the name changed with the year).

2. This is prior to July 1942, before all the non-Jewish residents of Terezín had been evacuated from the town. See Rabbi Erich Weiner, "*Freizeitgestaltung in Theresienstadt*," trans. Rebecca Rovit, in Rebecca Rovit and Alvin Goldfarb, eds., *Theatrical Performance during the Holocaust: Texts, Documents, Memoirs* (Baltimore: The Johns Hopkins University Press, 1999), 211.

3. Frýd, 207.

4. Letter to Rebecca Rovit, February 5 1998, reprinted in Rovit and Goldfarb, 230.

5. Klaus Leist, "Philipp Mane's: A Theresienstadt Chronicle," *The Journal of Holocaust Education*, 6, no 2 (1997): 51. Leist cites and translates Mane's original writing on pp. 319–20. Manes's journals were recently bequeathed to London's Wiener Library.

6. See Jana Sedová, "Theatre and Cabaret in the Ghetto of Terezín," in *Terezín*, 222.

7. Weiner, in Rovit and Goldfarb, 222. Josef Taussig suggests that the cabaret stars of the ghetto did not have to work heavy labor details. See Taussig, "Über die Theresienstädter Kabaretts," in *Theresienstädter Studien und Dokumente* (Prague: Theresienstädter Initiative im Verlag Academia, 1994), 214–46.

8. See Zdenka Ehrlich-Fantlová, "The Czech Theatre in Terezín," in Rovit and Goldfarb, 243. This is excerpted from Fantlová's memoir, *Klíd je síla, rek' tatínek* (Prague: Primus, 1996), also published in German as "*In der Ruhe liegt die Kraft,*" *sagte mein Vater* (Bonn: Weidle Verlag, 1999).

9. Památník Terezín (Terezín Memorial) has established a permanent exhibit in the former Magdeburg barracks dedicated to the theatrical activities of Theresienstadt. The Memorial also holds works by Zelenka. Sketches for set designs by Adolf Aussenberg and Bedřich Graus (1942–44) have also been preserved.

10. See H. G. Adler, *Theresienstadt: Das Antlitz einer Zwangsgemeinschaft* (Tübingen: J.C. B. Mohr, 1960); Zdenek Lederer, *Ghetto Theresienstadt* (New York: Howard Fertig, 1983).

11. Šedová, 219.

12. Ibid., 225.

13. Herbert Exenberger (deported February 7, 1943), "Vom 'Cabaret ABC im Regenbogen' zur 'Lindenbaum-Gruppe' in Theresienstadt," *Theresienstädter Studien und Dokumente,* (Prague, 1996), 241.

14. Weiner in Rovit and Goldfarb, 224. It was performed in attic A of the Hanover barracks. Paper hung on wires alongside the platform to darken the sides and allow for a dressing room space; four to five lamps served as spotlights. The audience had to stand mostly, except for two rows of benches reserved for the prominents.

15. The only operas which were fully staged—with sets by František Zelenka—were Pergolesi's *La Serva Padrona* (1944) in Czech and *Carmen* (1944), which was directed by Kurt Gerron. Franz Eugen Klein conducted the German-language operas.

16. Frýd , 213.

17. Weiner in Rovit and Goldfarb, 223.

18. Fantlová describes in detail her performances in "The Czech Theatre in Terezín" in Rovit and Goldfarb, 231–49.

19. The "Ghetto Swingers" under the direction of Martin Roman, later played in the coffeehouse that opened in December 1942. See Joža Karas, *Music in Terezín 1941–1945* (New York: Pendragon Press, Beaufort Books, 1985).

20. Taussig, 225–26.

21. See Ulrike Migdal, ed. *Und die Musik spielt dazu: Chansons und Satiren aus dem KZ Theresienstadt* (Munich: Piper, 1986), 67–70 for song about the Strauss family; English translation of "Theresienstadt Questions" by Roy Kift in Rovit and Goldfarb, 222.

22. Midgal, 28–9; Barbara Felsmann and Karl Prümm, *Kurt Gerron–Gefeiert und Gejagt: Das Schicksal eines deutschen Unterhaltungskünstlers* (Berlin: Edition Hentrich, 1992), 97.

23. Felsmann und Prümm, 99–101.

24. Taussig, 217, 226.

25. Taussig, 218. Taussig writes that the cabarets had no clear point of view towards the present, because no perspective existed for the future. The future (or remembered past) was only mentioned to draw attention to the present.

26. Ibid., 234. This was the Horpatsky and Porges cabaret.

27. Ludvík Vaclavek, "Zur Problematik der deutschen Lyrik aus Theresienstadt 1941–1945", in *Theresienstädter Studien und Dokumente* (Prague, 1994), 131. See also Taussig, 223.

28. Šedová, 221.

29. Taussig, 222–23.

30. Ibid., "The World from Above," 237–38.

31. Leist 55, cites Mane's original pages, 540–41.

32. Ibid., 48. Manes refers to a 1944 reading of *Urfaust* with actors Julius Arnfeld as a "fantastic" Faust and Friedrich Lerner as a "very modern" Mephisto.

33. Ibid., 65, cites Manes, 823–24 on a transport including actors Lerner, Dr. Bebol, Roth, Schoenfeld.

34. Gerty Spies, *My Years in Theresienstadt*, trans. Jutta Tragnitz (New York: Prometheus, 1997), 119.

35. From *"Karussell"* by Manfred Greiffenhagen, 1944. English translation courtesy of Roy Kift.

36. Vlasta Koubška, unpublished manuscript.

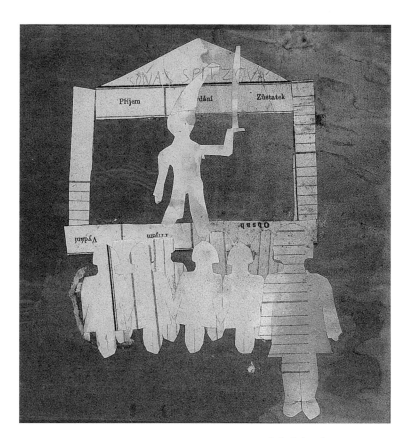

Soňa Spitzová
Collage
Born February 17, 1931
Deported to Terezín
December 10, 1941
Deported to Auschwitz
October 6, 1944
Perished
The Jewish Museum, Prague
#125.499

136

KURT GERRON AND HIS CABARET "KARUSSELL"

Charlotta Burešová
Pencil on paper
The Jewish Museum, Prague

Kurt Gerron

Kurt Gerron, born in 1897 as Kurt Gerson, was a German actor, cabaret star, and film director in Berlin in the 1920s and 1930s until the 1933 anti-Jewish boycott. He worked in Amsterdam in exile before his deportation to the Dutch transit camp, Westerbork. He was deported to Theresienstadt on February 25, 1944 and later deported to Auschwitz on October 28, 1944, whereupon he perished shortly after his arrival.

At Theresienstadt, Gerron established the German-language cabaret "Carousel" ("Karussell"). He sang and directed musical numbers from Berlin and also performed new theater skits.

He attracted writers, singers, and actors, from Vienna and Berlin to compose texts for the cabaret. Manfred Greiffenhagen (born 1896) has been credited with writing the cabaret theme song, "Carousel."

Greiffenhagen was deported to Terezín on January 27, 1944 and was deported to Auschwitz on October 12, 1944, where he perished.

Leo Strauss also wrote for Gerron's cabaret "Karussell." Strauss and his wife, Myra, (also a performer), had been deported from Vienna to Terezín on February 2, 1942. Strauss was transported to Auschwitz on September 28, 1944, and did not survive.

Zelenka's costume designs for the "Karussell" performers, Michel Gobets (tenor) and Anny Frey (soprano), suggest the high society of Vienna, Berlin, or Paris prior to the war. Many of the "Karussell" numbers nostalgically and ironically recalled the dress, customs, and dialects from these European cities.

František Zelenka
Flat designed for
Cabaret "Karussell"
The design of a Terezín window suggests the imprisoned world of Terezín inside the room (on stage) and outside the barred window. A recurring theme in many of the chanson texts is the clash between the memory of the world outside of Terezín and the reality inside the ghetto.
*National Museum,
Theater History Department
Prague #D5891*

František Zelenka
Flat designed for
Cabaret "Karussell"
*Extended View from
the Terezín Window*

As the imagination extends into the past or the future, so too does the view through the window. The distant scene through the archway reveals the sea. Visible boats suggest a means of departure (in the Terezín reality, the river Ohre). In this sketch, the sun has come out to replace the grey behind the window bars in the design above.

*National Museum,
Theater History Department
Prague #6755/52*

František Zelenka
Costume designs for
Cabaret "Karussell"

National Museum,
Theater History Department
Prague #6757/52

138

FRANTIŠEK ZELENKA

Zelenka was an influential architect, graphic designer, and and stage designer between the World Wars.

Zelenka was born in Kutná Hora in 1904. He was deported to Terezin on July 13, 1943. He was deported to Auschwitz on transport Es 1155 on October 19, 1944, where he perished.

In Terezín, Zelenka designed stage sets and costumes for more than twenty productions of plays, operas, and cabaret revues, not all of which were actually produced.

He worked in the cultural department, *Freizeitgestaltung*, together with both German and Czech-speaking artists.

It not known how Zelenka's scenic designs from Terezín were saved, but it is probable that his mother, Kamila Zelenka, who remained in Theresienstadt until liberation, was given his drawings for safekeeping. In 1952, she sold the majority of her son's stage and costume designs to the National Museum in Prague, where they remain today.[36]

František Zelenka
Costume design for
Cabaret "Karussell"
*National Museum,
Theater History Department
Prague #6758/52*

František Zelenka

THE LAST CYCLIST

Karel Švenk

The Last Cyclist was a satirical theatrical revue, allegorical in nature. The production was banned from its final performance by the Jewish Council of Elders before opening night because of the revue's cutting anti-Nazi message. Nevertheless, the play's rehearsals evidently had large audiences due to Švenk's established reputation for politically provocative cabaret. Immediately after censorship of *The Last Cyclist*, Švenk fashioned a new revue program in which he featured some of the songs from the forbidden *The Last Cyclist*. This revue was called *The Same but Different*.

Playwright and Director
Karel Švenk

František Zelenka
Stage and costume designer

Synopsis
In an imaginary country, all the psychopaths escape from their asylums and take over the government under the "Rat" dictator. The play's premise is that all cyclists are responsible for all the ills in the country. Because the cyclists are such a dangerous group of people, they are to be expelled. They are deported by ship to the Island of Horrors. One cyclist, Borivoj Abeles, survives. He falls off the ship, is then caught and exhibited in the zoo as the "last cyclist." The Rat-dictator decides to shoot him into space, but Borivoj Abeles outsmarts the Rat-dictator and his entourage. While they inspect the rocket, he asks permission to light a cigarette. He then lights the fuse of the rocket and the dictator and his entourage hurtle towards outer space.

František Zelenka
Scenic design for
The Last Cyclist
National Museum,
Theater History Department
Prague #6838/52

Sign reads,
"Entrance for
Naturalists."

140

BRUNDIBÁR OR THE ORGAN GRINDER

Johann (Hans) Krása
Composer

Adolf Hoffmeister
Librettist

Rudolf Freudenfeld
Director

František Zelenka
Set and stage designer

Rafael Schächter
Conductor

Brundibár, 1944
Still photograph from Nazi propaganda
film, *Theresienstadt: A Documentary Film
from the Jewish Settlement Area.*
*Collection of Ela Weissberger (shown in front
row in the black costume of "Cat").*

Terezín's premiere of *Brundibár* on September 23, 1943 was performed
in the Magdeburg barracks with a setting adapted from one used in the
original Prague orphanage. When the popular opera moved to the
Sokol Hall (which had a modern stage and orchestra pit), Zelenka had
to construct a new set with more color to please Commandant Rahm.

Rudolf Freudenfeld

BRUNDIBÁR

Synopsis

Two children, Pepiček and Aninka have a sick mother. There is not enough money to buy the milk for her. The children decide to sing like the organ-grinder, Brundibár, whom they have seen playing music for money. But Brundibár chases them away. The following day, with the help of some animals and school children, they sing to earn money but the organ-grinder steals their money. In the end, the children join together, get their money back, and celebrate their victory over Brundibár.

The opera, written and composed in 1938 in Prague, was also performed there by boys in an orphanage during the winter of 1942. The conductor Rafael Schächter was deported to Terezín in November 1942. In 1943 the composer Hans Krása, the stage designer František Zelenka, and the orphanage director, Moris Freudenfeld, and his son Rudolf arrived in the ghetto.

Schächter initiated a Terezín production of *Brundibár* directed by Rudolf Freudenfeld, who had directed the orphanage performance and brought the vocal score to the ghetto. Krása rewrote the opera score to include a variety of musical instruments. Rehearsals took place in Block L 417.

Ela Weissberger, who played the role of "Cat" in all fify-five performances, recalls that when the cast was onstage they were allowed to remove their stars.

František Zelenka
Set design used for *Brundibár*, 1943–44
Watercolor and ink on paper
Zelenka's design was originally created for Labiche's *The Straw Hat (Slameny kloubouk)* performed at the Osvobozene Theater in Prague during the 1930s.
National Museum, Theater History Department, Prague (S XIX a–5e)

Otto Ungar,
Hans Krása (detail)
Pencil on paper, n.d.
Collection of Joža Karas

Rebecca Rovit

142

ESTHER

Norbert Frýd
Director

Composer
Karel Reiner

Scenic and costume design
František Zelenka

Synopsis:
Esther was based on an old Czech folk play in archaic Czech verse as well as on the biblical story. Mordechai, a Jewish servant to the great Persian King, overhears a plot to kill the king and tells him. The King plans a banquet, but the queen refuses to attend. She is barred from the palace and her crown is taken away. The King then chooses a young Jewish virgin, Esther— Mordechai's niece. Meanwhile, he promotes his counselor, Haman, to minister. The counselor and his wife are greedy and power hungry—they expect all subjects to bow to them. Mordechai refuses and will only bow to the King. Haman decides to rid his kingdom of all the Jews, starting with Mordechai. Esther pleads on behalf of her uncle and of all Jews. The King thwarts Haman's plans and has Haman hanged.

Queen Vašta
was played by
Zdenka Fantlová

Costume design for Kat,
(The Executioner),
played by František Král

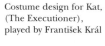

Costume design for
King Ahashuerus played
by Karel Kavan

František Zelenka
Costume designs for *Esther*
Watercolor and ink on paper
National Museum, Theater History Department, Prague
#6734/52; 5847/52;6735/52

ULLMANN-KIEN "ATLANTIS"

František Zelenka
Set design for *The Emperor of Atlantis: Death Abdicates*
Watercolor and ink on paper, 1944
Rehearsals for the one-act opera in four scenes had been completed in the Sokol Hall with its modern stage and orchestra pit.
National Museum, Theater History Department Prague #6706/52

EMPEROR OF ATLANTIS: DEATH ABDICATES

Viktor Ullmann
Composer

Petr Kien
Librettist

Rafael Schächter
Conductor

Karl Meinhard
Director

František Zelenka
Stage designer

Synopsis
The dictator of Atlantis, Emperor Overall (Überall), declares universal war. But death refuses to cooperate. So no one can die. As the forces of life against the Emperor converge, he begs Death to return. "Without you we people could not live," the Emperor tells Death. But Death will only return if the Emperor is the first to die. The small cast of five singers included the opera singer, Karel Berman for whom the role of death had been written.

Setting
This design could be used for all scenes which take place in Atlantis. Center stage is the omnipresent loudspeaker. To the far right is Emperor Overall's throne. Simple and abstract, the setting relies on draperies and simple wooden platforms which were probably moveable.

Born January 1, 1898
Deported to Terezín
September 8, 1942
Deported to Auschwitz,
October 16, 1944,
Perished
Ullmann was the son-in-law of Anton Dvořák.
Terezín Memorial #4780

Viktor Ullmann

Art, Music and Education as Strategies for Survival: Theresienstadt 1941–45

THE GENOCIDE OF THE CZECH JEWS
IN WORLD WAR II AND THE TEREZÍN GHETTO

Unknown Photographer
A Jewish worker moves confiscated property to a storage area in an unidentified warehouse., n.d.
The Jewish Museum Fotoarchiv, Prague #3.659

Nazi officials confiscated many items of value from Jewish homes, synagogues, and museums, including household china, art works, libraries, religious objects, folk art, furniture, clothing, and sundry other items involuntarily abandoned with the deportation of their owners. One hundred fifty-three Jewish communities from Bohemia and Moravia sent items to the Central Jewish Museum in Prague.

For the SS, these collections were to form the basis of a museum that would exhibit the culture of the "extinct Jewish race after the Final Solution had been completed." In September 1942, the SS allowed an exhibition of Jewish books and manuscripts to be displayed in the synagogues of the old town. The Jewish curators were permitted to restore the synagogue buildings and objects, thus enabling them to preserve their religious and cultural heritage.

Other exhibitions were held during the war, including one on Jewish life-cycle events and an exhibition of works by nineteenth-century Jewish artists. The curators and Jewish officials were simultaneously being deported and by 1944, the Central Jewish Museum had become a warehouse for Czech Jewish culture. This collection of objects eventually became the basis for the State Jewish Museum in Prague, created in 1950.

VOJTĚCH BLODIG

Unknown Photographers
pp 144–45, l–r: Warehouses for
confiscated paintings, household china,
and musical instruments, n.d.
*The Jewish Museum Fotoarchiv, Prague
l–r, pages 144–45, #1.155, 2.998, 2.878*

In the Czech lands occupied by Germany in early
1939, the Nuremberg definition of who was a
Jew was introduced in a decree about Jewish
property from the Reich Protector Konstantin
Freiherr von Neurath, issued June 21, 1939.
Foreign minister of Germany from 1932 to
1938 and later Reich Protector of Bohemia
and Moravia, von Neurath presided over anti-
Jewish activity. Von Neurath apathetically
cooperated with the Nazi program until he
was replaced. He was later sentenced at
Nuremberg to fifteen years in prison for
war crimes.

From that point on, whoever was a Jew or a half-
caste was judged in the Protectorate
according to this decree. The terms "Jewish
firm" and "Jewish company" were introduced
as well, describing targets for sweeping
"Aryanization" carried out by German firms
on the territory of the Protectorate—even
in cases of negligible Jewish involvement in
a factory or business. A business was considered Jewish not only if one of its owners
or trustees was Jewish, but also if he was found
to be "under crucial Jewish influence." This
concerned not only large and medium-size
properties, but all Jewish property in the end.
The property was expropriated, classified, and
finally given to German citizens.

Unknown Photographer
It is not known if the photograph
shows luggage going for transport or
carts with confiscated items., n.d.
*The Jewish Museum Fotoarchiv,
Prague #4.702*

In the spring of 1939, the Jewish religious communities in the Protectorate numbered 103,000 persons, while an additional 15,000 people met the definition of Jewishness according to the Nuremberg laws. To this group one can add several thousands Jewish immigrants from Germany and Austria (which had been annexed by Germany in March 1938) as well as those who had fled the Sudetenland—the border region where Jews were in great danger after its separation from Czechoslovakia and annexation by Germany—where only 2,000 of the original 30,000 Jews remained. In all, some 120,000 people lived in the territory of the Protectorate who, before long, would become subject to the "Final Solution of the Jewish Question," the Nazi plan to kill all the Jews of Europe, carried out by mobile killing squads, and by means of ghettos, concentration camps, and death camps.

The anti-Jewish policy of the Nazi occupation regime, supported by the government of the Protectorate, mainly concentrated, until the autumn of 1941, on excluding Jews from public and economic life and confiscation of their property. These measures began soon after von Neurath's decree on defining Jewishness.

During the first period of the occupation, the German authorities supported emigration of Jews, or more accurately, strove to exile as many of them as possible from their original places of residence. Prior to the definitive decision about the Final Solution—physical extermination—the Jews were forced in various ways to emigrate, to reduce their numbers in the territories ruled by the Nazis and at the same time, to give up all of their possessions for the "needs of the Reich."

To coordinate the actions of all authorities concerned and to secure leadership in Prague (according to the model of a similar office in Vienna), the Central Office for Jewish Emigration was established, directly subordinate to the Jewish Department of the Berlin central office of the Gestapo, which was headed by the infamous Adolf Eichmann. The head of the Prague office was Hans Günther, the leading ideologist of Nazi racist theory who published his tracts during the Third Reich. Günther regarded Jews as a racial impurity that threatened Aryan civilization and therefore must be obliterated. After World War II, he reissued his books as if the Final Solution had never occurred.

Unknown Photographer
Transport from Theresienstadt to Auschwitz-
Birkenau, passing through Bauschowitz, guarded
by armed police in Czech uniform. Note bystanders
in foreground and housewives at lower left.
December 1941–May 1943
The Jewish Museum Fotoarchiv, Prague #24.762

In August 1942, when the implementation of
  the Final Solution was already in full swing,
  the office was renamed the Central Office
  for the Settlement of the Jewish Question,
  a euphemistic, but basically accurate,
  description of the agency by which the
  genocide of Czech Jews would be carried out.

Emigration, albeit a difficult process that included
  the loss of all previous social, economic,
  and familial ties as well as the loss of all
  possessions, later turned out to have been
  a lucky fate for those who managed to leave.
  In all, there were 26,000 legal emigrants.
  Several thousand people, however, left the
  Protectorate illegally, many becoming
  members of Czechoslovak military units
  in the West and East. Many Jews faced
  persecution in a different way—they provided themselves with false papers and
  then lived illegally, many as active members
  of the Czech resistance movement.

On September 19, 1941, in the territory of the
  Protectorate as well as in all territories of the
  German Reich, the compulsory design-ation
  of all Jews over the age of six with a yellow
  star with the inscription "Jude" ("Jew") was
  decreed. This made it possible to control all
  people of Jewish origin, and to strengthen
  their segregation from the rest of the population. This was an essential part of the
  imminent preparations for the implementation of the next phase of the Final Solution.

The six-pointed Star of David worn on the left breast became mandatory on September 19, 1941 for all Jews above the age of six in the Reich (Germany, Austria, Sudentenland and the Protectorate of Bohemia-Moravia). The use of markings, such as the star, isolated and identified the intended victims from the surrounding population. Dutch Jews were required to wear the star after April 29, 1942. Danish Jews were not compelled to wear the star until after they arrived in Theresienstadt.

Star of David
Collection of Ela Weissberger

A series of clandestine photographs taken by Walter Weiss during his internment in Theresienstadt, 1942–45.
A camera was smuggled into the camp by Walter's Christian girlfriend. While Weiss was repairing the clock on the tower, shown at left, he took these photographs. The film and camera was kept by Weiss's girlfriend until after the war, when the film was developed. Walter Weiss survived.

Collection of Ela Weissberger

A foreshadowing of this was the compulsory registration of all Jews, that accounted for all future victims of the final stages of the genocide.

On July 31, 1941, Hermann Göring, Commander-in-Chief of the Luftwaffe, President of the Reichstag, Prime Minister of Prussia, and designated successor to Hitler, in his capacity as Chairman of the Council of Ministers for Defense, addressed a letter to Reinhard Heydrich ordering him to start all necessary measures for the implementation of the "Final Solution of the Jewish Question in all of Europe under German influence" ("*im deutschen Einflussgebiet in Europa*").

Heydrich was second in importance to Heinrich Himmler in the Nazi SS organization. Nicknamed "The Blond Beast" by the Nazis, and "Hangman Heydrich" by others, Heydrich was the leading planner of Hitler's Final Solution. In the autumn of 1941, Adolf Hitler himself ordered Himmler to clear the Reich and the Protectorate of Bohemia and Moravia of Jews, from West to East "as soon as possible." He expressly ordered them not to be deported into the General-Government but rather to the occupied areas and then handed over for "treatment" ("*Behandlung*") directly to the commanders of the individual *Einsatzgruppen* (mobile killing units).

A necessary condition for following this order was a favorable military situation. However, the situation was not as favorable as it had appeared in the first weeks and months after the opening of the campaign in the East; at the end of 1941 and the beginning of 1942, it became necessary to find temporary solutions which would make it possible to continue the plan already launched. In the first place, it had become obvious that it was first necessary to assemble the victims intended for annihilation in concentration and transit camps before deporting them further East; and also that extermination should proceed not only by mass execution, but also via newly established extermination camps.

According to Hitler's original ideas, the Jews from the Reich and the Protectorate of Bohemia and Moravia should have been deported in three months to ghettos and camps established on the Polish territory incorporated into Germany, and from there, in the spring of 1942, to places of extermination. That, however, met with opposition from the occupation authorities in the regions concerned, who claimed that the plan was not realistic. The death camps were still only in their planning and construction phases. It became obvious that prior to the "evacuation" of the Jews from the Czech

From 1941 to 1945, the Theresienstadt ghetto held Jewish deportees from the Protectorate of Bohemia and Moravia, Slovakia, Germany, Austria, the Netherlands, and Denmark. Of the more than 140,000 European Jews and some Jews in protected mixed marriages, 74,000 came from Bohemia and Moravia, 43,000 from Germany, 15,000 from incorporated Austria, almost 5,000 from the Netherlands, more than 400 from Denmark, about 1,500 from Slovakia, and about 1,000 from Hungary. About 88,000 temporary inhabitants of Theresienstadt were thus sent to their deaths in the East via this ghetto way station.

Aerial view of Theresienstadt
Terezín Memorial, Fotoarchiv #637

150

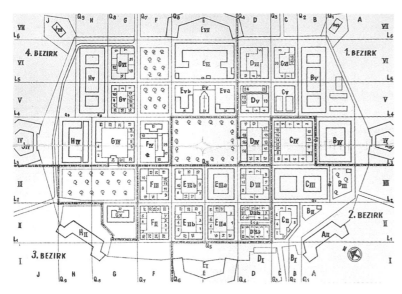

Map of Theresienstadt, including the town hall, church, and some of the former military barracks.

Leo Baeck Institute, New York
Copy courtesy United States Holocaust
Memorial Museum, w/s #75644

region (the euphemism employed to obscure the real substance of the Final Solution) for a certain time, "ghettoization" would be necessary on the territory of the Protectorate.

On September 27, 1941, Reinhard Heydrich was appointed Deputy Reich Protector of Bohemia and Moravia, replacing von Neurath. His arrival meant not only the escalation of the anti-Jewish measures, but also the first steps towards the practical implementation of the Final Solution on the territory of the Protectorate. Between October 16 and November 3, five transports with 5,000 deportees left for the Lodz Ghetto, the predominantly Jewish city in Poland that was transformed into a Jewish ghetto by the Nazis in 1941, followed on November 26 by a transport of 1,000 people to Minsk, a city in the German-occupied Soviet Union (today known as Belarus, or Byelorussia).

That was, however, only the beginning; early on, it became necessary to find an appropriate place for a concentration and transit camp. In a meeting held on October 10, 1941, presided over by Heydrich, it was decided that the camp for all of Bohemia and Moravia would be Terezín (Theresienstadt). The civilian population was ordered to leave Terezín and it was then assumed that after the completion of the deportation of Jews to

Helga Weissová-Hosková
A Transport of Polish Children
Watercolor and ink
August 29, 1943
Wallstein Verlag, Göttingen, Germany

extermination camps, the town would be converted into a model German settlement. Following another meeting on October 17, 1941, again chaired by Heydrich, organizational details of the "ghettoization" were deliberated, and it was decided that up to 60,000 Jews would be placed in the town that had formerly housed slightly more than 3,000 civilian inhabitants and about the same number of soldiers. Lamentably, less than a year later, that population level was actually attained.

Terezín was not chosen randomly; it was a former fortress with walls and moats that were easy to guard, and at the same time formed the boundaries of the camp. It also had several barracks buildings which could be used to house large numbers of prisoners. Also, the town was located within the Protectorate, surrounded largely by German territory and was only sixty kilometers from Prague. The main road to Dresden and Berlin passed through there, and the main railway line in the same direction was only three kilometers away. In nearby Litoměřice (Leitmeritz), there was a strong SS garrison as well as in the Small Fortress, only one kilometer away, which was converted into a police prison of the Prague Gestapo. So in case of an uprising by the prisoners, it would be possible swiftly to deploy strong forces for its suppression.

The history of the Terezín Ghetto proper began on November 24, 1941. That day, the so-called *Aufbaukommando* (construction work detail), consisting of 342 young men, arrived in the town. Their task was to prepare the Terezín barracks to receive transports which, after November 30, started arriving from all parts of the Protectorate. The first to arrive were transports from the large towns—Prague and Brno—and later from other points of concentration. Over time, more than 74,000 Czech Jews were transported to Terezín.

These children arrived in deplorable condition. During their entire stay in Theresienstadt they were in quarantine. When they were supposed to go into the showers they tried to resist and shouted 'GAS!' Even then they knew more than other inmates at Theresienstadt at that time.

For some reason they were supposed to be sent to Switzerland. That, however, never happened—they ended up in Auschwitz.

Helga Weissová-Hosková, drawing about the August 29, 1943, children's transport

Ivan Vojěch Fric
Dutch Jews on Theresienstadt street,
February 1944
United States Holocaust Memorial Museum
w/s #20258

Soon after its establishment, the Terezín Ghetto, in addition to its function as a concentration and transit camp, also served Nazi plans as a place of decimation, since a significant number of prisoners would die there as a result of insufferable living conditions. Early on, a third function was that of propaganda. For the Nazis, Terezín became a show town to camouflage the truth about the actual fate of the victims of the Final Solution and mass murder in the East.

On January 20, 1942, two months after the commencement of the deportations of the Czech Jews to Terezín, a conference of high German officials took place in the Berlin suburb of Wannsee, chaired by Reinhard Heydrich, which provided the Wannsee Protocol—further instructions for the implementation of the Final Solution already in progress. During the conference, Heydrich dealt with the difficulties arising from having to explain the deportation of old people to the East ostensibly for labor assignment, compounded by the high visibility of elderly veterans of World War I, holders of high distinctions and decorations, and people with strong international ties. To solve this problem, there needed to be, for a time, "old age ghettos." It was supposed that most prisoners would die there soon, and that also, as Heydrich stated, ". . . by that expedient solution, numerous interventions will be stopped immediately." The only old

age ghetto established was Terezín, where old people deported from the German Reich died en masse.

The first transport from Berlin arrived on June 2, 1942. Later, transports from other German-occupied territories arrived. In all, 140,000 people were forced into the Ghetto—74,000 from Bohemia and Moravia, 43,000 from Germany, 15,000 from Austria, 5,000 from the Netherlands, about 500 from Denmark, 1,500 from Slovakia and 1,000 from Hungary. These "regular" prisoners were joined, at the close of the war between April 20 and May 6, 1945, by approximately 15,000 prisoners who arrived in "evacuation" transports from the concentration camps in the East and North (evidence of which was being destroyed because of approaching Allied forces). In all, the total number of Jewish prisoners who passed through the Terezín Ghetto was approximately 155,000.

Transport to the Terezín Ghetto was only the beginning of the suffering they endured there. Many believed they could survive the camp. With this hope, they were able to endure lack of living space, malnutrition, hard work, epidemics and other aspects of everyday life. Individual prisoners were registered during their stay in Terezín under their transport numbers. Dormitories were frequently overcrowded to catastrophic dimensions, while ever-present and never-ending hunger, insufficient hygiene and systematic terror by the SS were basic features of life in the Ghetto.

Until the end of 1942, three-quarters of the Jewish population living in the Protectorate before the start of the deportation in autumn 1941 were forcibly "ghettoized" in Terezín. Starting in early 1943, the influx of prisoners from the Protectorate slowed but continued until March 1945. The total number of transports from the Protectorate numbered 122.

Prisoners' hopes that Terezín would be a place where life and work would be possible throughout the war, albeit under hard conditions, soon evaporated. As early as January 9, 1942, the first transport eastward left Terezín for Riga, in Nazi-occupied Latvia, followed by another sixty-two transports. These regular transports carried more than 87,000 people to places of mass extermination and to concentration camps. Of those transported, roughly 3,800 (three and one-half percent) survived to see the liberation.

Helga Weissová-Hosková
The Sluice in the Courtyard I
Watercolor and ink,
September 9, 1943
*Wallstein Verlag,
Göttingen, Germany*

The people included in the transports on arrival and departure were assembled in so-called 'sluices.'

The Czech word *Šlojska* was only used in the slang coined in Theresienstadt. The expression was derived from the German word *Schleuse*. Here, people were registered and checked. They had to wait for hours or days in heat and cold until they were called.

Helga Weissová-Hosková, 1943

Unknown Photographer
Courtyard of Dresden barracks in Theresienstadt,
taken shortly after liberation in May 1945
Czechoslovak News Agency, Copy courtesy
United States Holocaust Memorial Museum, w/s #40209

The eastbound transports, also called "Polish transports," became the nightmare of every prisoner. Although nothing was yet known of mass murder in the East, everybody guessed that in the East, chances of survival were much lower compared with Terezín. In 1942 in particular, when transports were leaving in short intervals, the tension among the prisoners was unbearable. Between January 9 and September 8, twenty-three transports left Terezín. Their destinations included, in Poland, Izbica Lubelska, Piaski, Lublin, Warsaw, Zamosc, Rejowiec Fabryczny, Trawniki, Sobibor, Ossowa, Majdanek and Vjazdow; in Byelorussia, Minsk, Maly Trostinec and Baranovici; Riga in Latvia; and and Raaiski in Estonia. The destination of transport AAi, dispatched eastwards at the time of the Nazi retaliation for the assassination of Reinhard Heydrich, is unknown even today.

The prisoners in these transports were, in overwhelming majority, massacred immediately upon arrival at their destination. Only a few were selected for labor; of 23,000 people only 229 survived this way, barely one percent. Transport AAy, dispatched from Terezín on July 28, 1942, was originally heading for Maly Trostinec, but because the SS staff there were "overworked" (as a report stated), all of the 1,000 prisoners had to get off at Baranovici, where they were immediately annihilated near the village of Kopelnice.

Another wave of eastbound transports followed in the period between September 19 and October 22, 1942. This time, the Nazis were attempting to relieve overcrowding in the Terezín Ghetto. Some 19,000 elderly people from the Protectorate were included in eleven transports; only three survived. One of these transports was dispatched to Maly Trostinec, while the rest were sent to the death factory at Treblinka, where between 700,000 and 860,000 Jews were killed.

In October 26, 1942, the first transport left for a new destination—Birkenau, a principal sub-camp of Auschwitz that operated four gas chamber centers that murdered 6,000 daily. From that point on, with the exception of two small transports to Bergen-Belsen, located in northwestern Germany near the town of Celle, all transports from Terezín were sent to Birkenau. In the first stage of deportation, between October 26, 1942, and February 1, 1943, 8,867 people were deported there, of whom only 124 survived (less than one and one-half percent). After that, a break of more than seven months ensued, which for most Terezín prisoners induced the hope that transports would stop completely.

In reality—as SS Chief Heinrich Himmler himself asserted—the objective was to preserve the perception in world opinion that Terezín was a place where "Jews could live and die in peace." After the Nazi defeat at Stalingrad

Unknown Photographer
A women with a basin of water, possibly washing clothing, her possessions and bedroll stacked on a bunk bed in Theresienstadt, 1941–45.
YIVO Institute for Jewish Research, Copy courtesy United States Holocaust Memorial Museum w/s #40218

HelgaWeissová-Hosková
Cutting Down Bunks
Watercolor and ink, 1944
Wallstein Verlag, Göttingen, Germany

Before the arrival of the International Red Cross Commission, a so-callled 'Beautifi-cation of the Town' took place." One of the projects included cutting down the third tier of bunks in the ground-floor rooms where the Commission could possibly see the overcrowded dormitories.

Helga Weissová-Hosková, drawing about the 1944 Red Cross visit to Theresienstadt

Ivan Vojěch Fric
Transport of arriving Dutch Jews receive
their first meal in the ghetto courtyard
Since it is late February 1944, they all wear
coats and hats for warmth.
United States Holocaust Memorial Museum
w/s #20266

and a series of further German military
setbacks, it was imperative to intensify the
propaganda camouflage. For that reason, the
odious "beautification" of Terezín was begun
for a brief period for the occasion of two
visits by delegations of the International
Committee of the Red Cross, and for the
production of a documentary propaganda
film.

The Nazis, however, had never seriously considered
stopping the deportations and exempting
Terezín prisoners from the murderous
transports. On September 6, 1943, a new
series of deportations to the East was started,
lasting until May 18, 1944; in all, 17,517
people were transported to Birkenau during
that period. In a change of Nazi policy,
newcomers from Terezín underwent no
transport selection, and whole families were
allowed to remain together in the "Terezín
family camp," section BIIb in Birkenau.
It is highly probable that the Nazis were
preparing a presentation of a "Jewish model
labor camp" to an international delegation;
no such visit materialized, the camp was no
longer needed, and most of the prisoners
were gassed or sent to various labor camps.
1,167 people from section BIIb survived
(six and one-half percent).

The last series of deportations to the East
started on September 28, 1944. In eleven

"liquidation transports," 18,402 prisoners were taken to Birkenau, of which 1,574 (8.5 percent) survived. The last of these transports, denoted Ev, was the last to undergo selection on the odious Birkenau ramp. Of its 2,038 prisoners, 1,689 were led straight to the gas chambers. Shortly afterwards, the equipment was dismantled and the individual buildings were blown up. The eastbound transports from Terezín were then stopped; however more Jews and "half-castes" were deported to Terezín until the spring of 1945.

In the last days of the war, evacuation transports brought to Terezín thousands of prisoners from liquidated Nazi camps in the East and North that were close to front-line fighting. Even after the liberation of Terezín by the Soviet Army on May 8, 1945, hundreds of former prisoners died from typhus and spotted fever. These were the final days of the Nazis' "model" Ghetto.

Egon Redlich, the head of the department for youth care in the Jewish Self-Government, who was sent to Terezín from Prague in 1941 and was transported to Auschwitz in 1944, noted in his diary with bitterness before his deportation to death in the East: ". . . a privileged Ghetto. . . a cloak for blood and victims in the East. A privileged Ghetto, where daily, over a hundred people die."

Kurt Jelenkiewicz
Pencil on paper
Born December 4, 1931
Deported to Terezín
October 24, 1942
Deported to Auschwitz
October 10, 1944
Perished
*The Jewish Museum, Prague
#135.028*

158

► Unknown Artist
Concert program,
1943
Terezín memorial #SOPT4200

▼ Unknown Photographer
Still of concert musicians from
the Nazi propaganda film,
*Theresienstadt: A Documentary Film
from the Jewish Settlement Area,*
August 1944
*Bildarchiv Preussischer Kulturbesitz,
Berlin #NS806a*

...the key to cultural survival was music. Three great Czech Jewish musicians were concentrationaires: conductor Rafael Schächter, [Gideon] Klein who later died in Auschwitz, and Karel Ancerl, who survived.... The most symbolic performance in the whole history of Terezín was, of course, Verdi's Requiem, conducted by Schächter in September 1944, after the Red Cross inspection of the camps. The Requiem was first performed for the visiting guests as part of the "Potemkin villages" sham. The last performance, however, was mounted when the German order of the ensuing transports was already known.

Only with these gruesome facts in mind is it possible to properly appreciate the history of the extraordinary cultural life of Terezín, for many the most powerful symbol of the "model Ghetto." Transports brought scores of people from many European countries; among them were leading personalities from various areas of Europe's intellectual life.

Amidst the specific conditions within the forcibly created community of Terezín, this mixture often produced unusually rich cultural activity, incomparable to anywhere else in war-torn Europe. The attitude of many Nazis on this issue was wholly pragmatic and cynical: "Let them play," was known to have been a standard response to the arts at Terezín. The Nazis knew that for all prisoners, their death sentences had already been passed, and only the time of the execution was uncertain.

Hence they gave considerable freedom to the prisoners' cultural activities. Their tolerance was meant to both contribute to the preservation of calm in Terezín, the "waiting room for Auschwitz," and to support their international propaganda program.

For the Terezín prisoners themselves, cultural endeavor played a very significant role in their effort to preserve personal integrity even under the conditions of imprisonment, as well as a way to fortify their belief in the future of

Mirko Tuma, "Memories of Theresienstadt,"
in Rebecca Rovit and Alan Goldfarb, eds.,
*Theatrical Performances during the Holocaust: Texts,
Documents, Memoirs* (Baltimore, 1999), 269

the Jewish people after the war. For these reasons their works often found extraordinary resonance, carrying the message of the just fight against violence, and a belief in the victory of good over evil. The children's opera *Brundibár* by composer Hans Krása and writer Adolf Hoffmeister, which was performed many times during and since the time of the Ghetto, contains a finalé about the defeat of the villain, which became a kind of hymn of the Terezín Ghetto.

After the war, the children's drawings from Terezín became world famous. The overwhelming majority of their authors—the youngest prisoners of the Ghetto—did not survive the war. Many of their drawings, however, remained hidden until after the war and

Even in the gloomy circumstances a place and time could be found for entertainment. This helped us escape for a while from the harsh reality.

Helga Weissová-Hosková, 1942

Gideon Klein (sitting in center) and an unidentified group of musicians
Terezín Memorial Fotoarchiv, #A1984

Helga Weissová-Hosková
Concert in the Dormitory
Watercolor and ink, 1942
*Wallstein Verlag,
Göttingen, Germany*

Unknown Photographer
Confiscated pianos, n.d.
The Jewish Museum Fotoarchiv, Prague #2.870

Art, Music and Education as Strategies for Survival: Theresienstadt 1941–45

endure today as a lasting warning about regimes of violence, as well as an appeal for active defense of democratic rights.

With their simple beauty, reflecting the pure souls of children, the children's drawings from Terezín are possibly the most expressive comment on the monstrous crime of the Final Solution. The real dimensions of that crime have long been suppressed in the Czech Republic; the reasons, political and ideological, are well known. The distortion of history which was the consequence of suppression unfortunately has found its reflection in the historical consciousness of, in particular, our younger generation. Consequently it should be the preeminent task of Czech historiography to eliminate the debt left open in this field by the forty years of the Communist regime.

Kurt Wurzel
Pencil on paper
Born May 6, 1932
Deported to Terezín
September 26, 1942
Deported to Auschwitz
October 23, 1944
Perished
The Jewish Museum, Prague
#135.028

Unknown Artist
Terezín Fortress
Watercolor, n.d.
Painted on the lid of
a sugar box (shown at right)
Signed "J.M. Coon" or "Coan"

Simon Wiesenthal Museum of Tolerance,
Los Angeles

Note: "Terezín" is used for the geographic place name then and today, and "Theresienstadt" for the ghetto during the period 1941–45.

162

1938	**October 1**	Germany occupies the Sudetenland.
	October 6	An autonomous government is established in Slovakia.
1939	**March 15**	Germany occupies Bohemia and Moravia.
	March 16	The Reich Protectorate of Bohemia and Moravia is established; Subcarpathian Ruthenia is ceded to Hungary.
	June 21	A decree defines "Jews," based on the Nuremberg racial laws. New regulations are enacted for the registration and liquidation of property and assets owned by Jews in the Protectorate. The Germans open Hadega (*Handelsgesellschaft*) in Prague to register gold, platinum, and silver articles, and jewelry owned by Jews.
	July	The Central Office for Jewish Emigration (*Zentralstelle für jüdische Auswanderung*) is opened in Prague under the supervision of Adolf Eichmann.
	July 4	Jewish students are excluded from German-language public schools and high schools in the Protectorate. Jewish students in Czech-language schools are restricted to four percent *numerus clausus* of all matriculated students.
	August 11	Jews in provincial areas of the Protectorate are ordered to leave their homes and resettle in Prague within one year.
	August 14	A police decree prohibits Jews from using most restaurants and cafes. Subsequent prohibitions forbid Jews from using public swimming and sports facilities. Hospitals and homes for the aged are ordered to segregate Jewish and non-Jewish patients.
	September 1	Germany invades Poland.
1940	**January 26**	A decree mandates the "elimination of Jews from the Protectorate economy," resulting in the "Aryanization" or liquidation of "Jewish enterprises."
	February 20	The Protectorate Administration in Prague excludes Jews from attending theater performances and movies.
	April 9	Germany occupies Denmark and invades Norway.
	April 22	The Gestapo imposes a curfew between 8pm and 6am on Jews in the Protectorate.
	May 10	Germany invades Western Europe.
	May 14	The Netherlands surrenders to Germany.

SYBIL H. MILTON

May 17		Prague police prohibit Jews from using public parks and gardens in the city.
May 28		Belgium surrenders to Germany.
June 22		France surrenders to Germany.
October 10		The Prague municipal administration decrees that Jews will not receive ration cards for clothing.

1941

January 18 — The Protectorate Department of Agriculture refuses to issue Jews ration cards for apples. By 1942, these restrictions expand to includes prohibitions on receiving rations of sugar, vegetables, fruits, meat, fish, poultry, diary products, soap, and tobacco products.

June 22 — Germany invades the Soviet Union.

September 6 — Jews are prohibited from using public libraries and lending libraries in the Protectorate. This decree is expanded on December 4, 1941, to include museums, exhibitions, galleries, and archives.

September 19 — All Jews above the age of six in the Reich, including the Protectorate, are ordered to wear a six-pointed yellow Star of David, with the word "*Jude*" ("Jew") in black calligraphy. Section 3 of this decree exempt *Mischlinge* (part-Jews) and Jews with non-Jewish spouses holding German citizenship from wearing the Star. Czech Jews married to non-Jews are not exempt.

1942

February 21 — Prague police headquarters prohibits Jews from using laundries and cleaners.

July 24 — All Jewish schools are closed in the Protectorate and on July 27, the Protectorate Department of Education prohibits private lessons for Jewish children by paid or unpaid teachers. On September 8, 1942, *Mischlinge* of the first degree (nonpracticing half-Jews with two Jewish grandparents not married to Jews) are barred from German and Czech language educational institutions, although they are still allowed in vocational, agricultural, and art schools with special permission issued by the Department of Education.

THERESIENSTADT

1941

October 10 — Reinhard Heydrich, Adolf Eichmann, and six other members of the Nazi occupation staff meet in Prague to discuss the "solution of the Jewish problem" for the Protectorate. They decide to convert Terezín into a ghetto for Jewish deportees en route to the East.

October 17	Second meeting in Prague under the chairmanship of Reinhard Heydrich proposes the Theresienstadt ghetto as an assembly and transit camp for the Jews from the Protectorate.
November 24	The first transport, AKI, with 342 Jewish men from Prague, arrives in Theresienstadt as a construction labor detail (*Aufbaukommando*).
November	SS First Lieutenant Dr. Siegfried Seidl is appointed the first commandant of the Theresienstadt ghetto. He stays at this post until July 3, 1943.
November 30– December 4	The first large transports of Jews from Prague, including the elderly, arrive in Theresienstadt.
December 6	Women and children are housed separately from men in the Dresden barracks.

1942

January 9	First transport (transport O) departs Theresienstadt for the Riga ghetto. This is the first transport to the East.
January 20	At the Wannsee conference, Theresienstadt is designated as an *Altersghetto*, a destination for elderly Jews and those with connections from Germany and Austria. The October 1941 transports to the Litzmannstadt ghetto included large numbers of Jews over the age of sixty-five, and this fact could not be harmonized with the contention that the Jews are being sent East to do heavy labor. Theresienstadt becomes a way station for elderly German and Austrian Jews en route to the East serving to hide from the populace the radical nature of these deportations, setting in motion the deadly deception that made Theresienstadt the symbol of Nazi duplicity.
February 16	Reinhard Heydrich, deputy Protector, decrees that the town of Theresienstadt be dissolved. All 3,142 original inhabitants of Terezín are ordered to move by June 30, 1942.
April	The first transport of 1,000 Jewish men, women, and children from Theresienstadt arrives in Trawniki en route to the ghetto and transit camp at Piaski in Poland. Approximately 350 young men from this transport are sent to Majdanek concentration camp and gassed there.
April 25	The first transport of 1,000 Jews is sent from Theresienstadt to Warsaw. Those judged fit for labor are sent to Rembertów labor camp near Warsaw; those considered unfit for labor are deported and killed in Treblinka. Only eight men survive this transport.

April 29	The SS Police Leader in the Netherlands issues a decree ordering all Dutch Jews to wear the yellow star with a black imprint "*Jood*" ("Jew").
May 17	The first transport leaves Theresienstadt for Lublin.
May 27	Reinhard Heydrich, head of the Central Office for Reich Security (RSHA) and Protector of Bohemia and Moravia, is severely injured in an ambush near Prague by Czech partisans (he subsequently dies from this injury).
June 2	The first transport of Jews from Berlin arrives in Theresienstadt.
June 10	Ghetto commandant Seidl orders thirty men deported from Theresienstadt to Lidice, where they are ordered to prepare a mass grave for those killed (199 male residents over the age of fifteen) in the village of Lidice in reprisal for Heydrich's assassination.
June 21	The first transport of Austrian Jews from Vienna arrives in Theresienstadt.
July	The children's homes L410 for Czech girls ages eight to sixteen, where Friedl Dicker-Brandeis taught, and L417 for Czech boys ages ten to fifteen, where the magazine *Vedem* was produced, are opened in Theresienstadt.
August 1	Prison camps for Roma and Sinti (Gypsies) at Lety and Hodonin in the Protectorate are changed into concentration camps by an Interior Ministry decree.
August 3	The Germans order work on a permanent exhibition at the Central Jewish Museum in Praguc on Jewish cultural and religious life. The Germans consider this as "gathering relics of an extinct Jewish race;" the Jews ordered to work on this exhibition perceive it as a way of preserving their religious and cultural objects for posterity.
August 14	Construction begins on a three kilometer rail spur connecting Bauschowitz (Bohusoviče) with the Theresienstadt ghetto.
September 7	A crematorium is built in Theresienstadt and all four ovens are in use by October 1942. The dead are buried in individual graves until August 1942; thereafter, mass graves are dug to hold up to thirty-six coffins. After October 1942, the ashes of deceased prisoners are stored in urns and marked for identification. (Cremation is forbidden in Jewish religious tradition).
September 18	The Jewish population of Theresienstadt reaches its high point of 58,491. During the month of September, inadequate shelter, hygiene, and food result in the death of 3,941 ghetto inmates.

October 26	The first transport is sent from Theresienstadt to Auschwitz-Birkenau. Between October 1942 and late October 1944, a total of twenty-five transports with more than 44,000 prisoners are deported to Auschwitz-Birkenau, where most are killed.
December 8	A café, seating approximately 100 people, is opened daily from 10 am to 5:30 pm in house Q418. A pass enables a prisoner to stay there up to two hours; music and cabaret are performed at the café.
January 20–26	Mass deportations from Theresienstadt to Auschwitz-Birkenau.
February 2	A seven months pause in deportations to the East from February 2 to September 5, 1943, results in stabilization of ghetto life. The total prisoner population is approxiamately 44,672.
April 22	The first Jewish transport from the Netherlands arrives at Theresienstadt from Westerbork.
June 1	The first train from Bauschowitz to Theresienstadt arrives on the newly completed rail spur. Up to that date, Jewish deportees were forced to march the 2.8 kilometer distance to the ghetto.
July 3	SS Lieutenant Colonel Anton Burger replaces Seidl as commandant of Theresienstadt, and serves until February 7, 1944. The Sudeten and Bodenbach barracks are cleared of Czech prisoners to accomodate the archives of the Central Office for Reich Security (RSHA) that had been moved from Berlin to evade Allied bombing. The removal of the archives to Theresienstadt signals the arrival of a considerable number of German officials and their families in the ghetto.
August 24	Dr. Wilhelm Frick is appointed Reich Protector of Bohemia and Moravia.
August 25	A transport with 1,260 children from the liquidated Bialystok ghetto arrives in Theresienstadt. These children are held in isolation and on October 5, together with fifty-three Theresienstadt inmates who were assisting them, they are deported to Auschwitz-Birkenau.
September 5	Transports Dl and Dm transport 5,007 Theresienstadt prisoners to the "Theresienstadt family camp," BIIb, at Auschwitz-Birkenau. The "family camp" eventually holds approximately 17,517 Jews from Thersienstadt between September 1943 and mid-July 1944; only 1,167 survive to liberation.

1943

Initially at BIIb, the Theresienstadt prisoners are allowed to keep their civilian clothing, their hair was not cut off, and families are permitted to remain together although the barracks are separated by gender. The life expectancy of each transport group is about six months.

One of the most poignant acts of resistance is committed by 3,971 Czech Jews, who on March 8, 1944, suspecting they would be gassed, begin singing the Jewish anthem "Hatikvah" as well as the Czech national anthem. The SS kill all but thirty-seven of them on this day.

October 5   The first transport of Danish Jews arrives in Theresienstadt.

December 15–18   An additional 5,007 persons are deported from Theresienstadt to the Auschwitz-Birkenau "Theresienstadt family camp."

December   On RSHA orders "beautification" of Theresienstadt for possible international visitors begins.

1944

January 20   Filming of an arriving Dutch transport in Theresienstadt.

February 8   SS First Lieutenant Karl Rahm is appointed as the third and last commandant of Theresienstadt and serves in this function until the end of the war.

June 23   An International Red Cross delegation, comprised of two Danish officials and one Swiss representative, inspect the Theresienstadt ghetto. Their visit lasts six hours. The prisoners were instructed on how to behave during this inspection and are compelled to give positive reports about ghetto conditions.

July 17   Several Jewish artists (including Leo Haas, Otto Ungar, Bedřich Fritta, Karel Fleischmann, and Norbert Troller) are arrested for distributing "atrocity propaganda" in their artwork. They are transferred to the police prison in the Small Fortress at Theresienstadt, which is under the jurisdiction of the Prague Gestapo. After brutal interrogations and beatings, many are deported to Auschwitz in October 1944. Only Leo Haas and Norbert Troller survived to see the liberation.

August 16   A camera crew from the Prague newsreel company Aktualita is ordered to shoot a propaganda film (*Theresienstadt: Ein Dokumentarfilm aus dem judischen Siedlungsgebict*) about Theresienstadt. The SS appoints the German Jewish prisoner Kurt Gerron, a Berlin actor and cabarettist, to head the Jewish production team, that also includes the Czech Jewish architect František Zelenka, and the Dutch Jewish artist Jo Spier, who makes hundreds of little sketches during the film shooting. Film work is complete September 11, 1944.

August 29	The Slovak National uprising begins.
September 28	A series of eleven liquidation transports between September 28 and October 28 from Theresienstadt to Auschwitz-Birkenau result in the deportation of more than 18,000 prisoners. About 11,000 prisoners remain in Theresienstadt, including about 819 children under the age of fifteen.
November 11	Theresienstadt commandant Rahm orders the destruction of urns containing the ashes of deceased Jews. Prisoners are informed that the ashes will be buried in the Prague Jewish cemetery; however, they are dumped into the Ohre (Eger) river and are also buried near the concentration camp at Litoměřice (Leitmeritz).
November 26	Heinrich Himmler orders the dismantling of gas chambers and crematoriom in Auschwitz-Birkenau; surviving prisoners are transferred to concentration camps in the German Reich and to the Theresienstadt ghetto.
December 23	The first transport of Slovakian Jews from the Sered labor and internment camp arrives in Theresienstadt. Additional transports arrive in January, March, and April 1945.

1945

January 31	Transports of several thousand German and Czech Jews in mixed marriages and part Jews (*Mischlinge*), who had previously been protected, begin to arrive in Theresienstadt.
February 5	A transport of 1,200 Jews is released from Theresienstadt and departs for Switzerland, reaching the Swiss border on February 7.
February	The construction of a gas chamber begins in Theresienstadt.
March 5	Theresienstadt is visited by Adolf Eichmann, who orders a new "beautification" of the ghetto because of negotiations between RSHA chief Ernst Kaltenbrunner and the International Red Cross about the inspection and possible rescue of concentration camp inmates.
April 4	Bratislava, the capital of Slovakia, is liberated.
April 6	Paul Dunant of the International Red Cross Committee, accompanied by Eichmann, visits Theresienstadt.
April 15	Swedish Red Cross buses remove 423 Danish prisoners from Theresienstadt for transfer to Sweden.

April 20	The first transport of 2,000 prisoners evacuated from eastern concentration camps arrive in Theresienstadt. During the next two weeks, about 15,000 prisoners arrive in Theresienstadt. A typhus epidemic begins. By April 20, of the 17,238 prisoners in Theresienstadt, nearly thirty-six percent (converts and part-Jews) are not Jewish. Nearly 2,000 Catholics, Protestants, and unaffiliated persons are incarcerated in the ghetto during the last months.
May 2	The International Red Cross Committee assumes control of Theresienstadt and the Small Fortress.
May 5	The last SS men leave Theresienstadt.
May 8	The first Soviet Army tanks reach Theresienstadt en route to Prague. Approximately 30,000 prisoners, including persons on newly arriving evacuation transports from other camps, are liberated in Theresienstadt.
May 10	The Soviet Army assumes control of Theresienstadt.
May 28	The first repatriations of former prisoners from Theresienstadt occurs. Repatriations are complete by the end of August 1945.

SOURCES

American Jewish Committee, *The Jewish Communities of Nazi-occupied Europe,* prepared by the Research Institute on Peace and Postwar Problems. American Jewish Committee,1944; reprint,(New York: Howard Fertig, 1981), see chapter "The Jews of Czechoslovakia."

Avigdor Dagan, ed., *The Jews of Czechoslovakia: Historical Studies and Surveys,* vol. 3 (Philadelphia: Jewish Publication Society, 1984).

Miroslav Karny, Vojtěch Blodig, and Margita Karna, eds., *Theresienstadt in der "Endlösung der Judenfrage"* (Prague: Panorama, 1992).

170

REDEFINING CHILDHOOD

Soon after the Nazis gained power in Germany, Jewish children and children in mixed marriages found life increasingly difficult. Their parents had lost jobs and businesses and Jewish families became indigent because of legislation prohibiting Jews and non-Aryans from employ-ment in various professions.

Jewish children were prohibited from participating in sports and social activities with their "Aryan" classmates and neighbors.

Between 1933 and 1938, Jews were prohibited in museums, movies, public playgrounds, and public swimming pools. Even when Jewish children were permitted to continue in public schools, their teachers and classmates often treated them with indifference or contempt. Frequently, they were taunted, humiliated, picked upon, and even beaten up. In November 1938, Jewish children were expelled from German schools and forced into segregated schools.

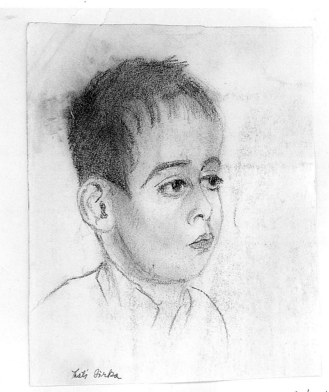

Jirka, was a boy of 5, sub letting my bed in the hospital. The poor children had smallpox in their hospital, so they had to evacuate it and having no space anywhere, they shared beds of other grown-up patients in other hospitals, for some days. Jirka was very gay and clever companion, but did not at all dislikes in one bed. Nobody could answer his 1000 questions.

Norbert Troller
Portrait of Jirka
Pencil on paper
Theresienstadt,
Fall 1943
nb: Troller's English description of "Jirka"
was added during the 1970s when he was writing his memoirs.
Estate of the artist, Doris Rauch; Troller Collection, Leo Baeck Institute, New York

SYBIL H. MILTON

> ...what could have happened to him had he survived?
>
> Norbert Troller
> Yeshiva University Museum, ed., *Terezín 1942–1945,*
> *Through the Eyes of Norbert Troller* (New York, 1981), 29–30

Jewish students in a classroom *JMP # 4512*

Norbert Troller completed more than 300 paintings and drawings in Theresienstadt, including six portraits of children. One of these portraits is entitled *Jirka*.

In translating his memoirs from Czech into English in the 1970s, Troller noted: "Jirka was my neighbor in the hospital. I was very weak after a lengthy operation and Jirka was recovering from an appendectomy. He never stopped talking or asking questions. At first, I was too tired to pay attention or to answer him. As I recovered, I started talking with him and answering his queries. His questions were sometimes very searching, often unexpected, original and funny, that many times I had to laugh to cover up my inability to answer them. Jirka became a cheerful, tireless nuisance, but I couldn't help loving him and he knew it.

"When I felt better and could draw again, I drew two sketches of him. Nobody can imagine the patience it took and how many stories and jokes I needed to keep him still for more than a minute.

"A few months later, he and his family were taken away in a transport and I never saw any of them again. I missed him as I missed too many of my close friends and relatives who disappeared in boxcars."

Yeshiva University Museum, ed., *Terezin 1942–1945, Through the Eyes of Norbert Troller* (New York, 1981), 29–30

Hana Wagnerová *JMP #33.206/1*

Art, Music and Education as Strategies for Survival: Theresienstadt 1941–45

These photographs were collected from family members, relatives or friends who survived. They were taken before transport to Theresienstadt. Most of these young people perished.

AN ALBUM OF CHILDREN TRANSPORTED TO THERESIENSTADT

Jiri Bleier JMP #21.832/1

Gertruda Eisingerová JMP #37.429

Vera Segerová JMP #29.995/1

Eva Glaserová JMP #32.034/1

Vladimir Flusser JMP #32.933/1

Marie Castelinová JMP #33.877

Child of the Popper family JMP #33.898

Sources for photographs on pages 171–77

TM   *Terezín Memorial*
JMP   *The Jewish Museum, Prague*
USHMM *United States Holocaust Memorial Museum*

It is believed that as many as 12,000 children under the age of eighteen had been deported to Theresienstadt. About 1,560 of them below the age of fifteen, or who had reached the age of fifteen in Theresienstadt, survived at liberation.

Helenka Popper *TM #8814*

Wally Tausigová with her niece Hana *TM #A8475*

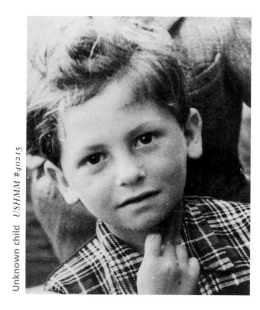

Unknown child *USHMM #40215*

174

With the incorporation of Austria in 1938 and the occupation of Bohemia and Moravia in 1939, the same restrictions extended to Jewish families and children living in these two countries.

With the outbreak of war in September 1939, life became much harder for children throughout Europe. They suffered from displacement, inadequate diets, the absence of fathers and brothers, loss of family members, trauma, and confusion. However, only certain groups of children were singled out for additional persecution.

Among the first victims were disabled persons in Germany and children were not exempt. Although some of the children killed in the first phase of the so-called "euthanasia" operation were Jewish, most of the children killed by lethal injection or asphyxiated by inhaling carbon monoxide into sealed mobile vans and gas chambers were non-Jewish German and Austrian children.

In Germany, Austria, and the Protectorate of Bohemia and Moravia, Nazi officials confiscated many items of value from Jewish homes, including radios, telephones, cameras, bicycles, and cars. Food rations and clothing ration cards were also curtailed for Jews. The Jewish children felt increasingly isolated.

By 1942, children along with their families were confronted by deportations to ghettos, concentration camps, and killing centers. Suffocating heat in the summer and freezing temperatures in winter made the deportation journey brutal. During these deportation trips, which usually lasted several days, there was no food or water, except for what people brought with them. Parents were powerless to defend their children.

It was rare for entire Jewish families to survive. Usually one or more of the parents were likely to have been killed along with grandparents. For children in Theresienstadt, as well as in other settings, the present was insecure and the future uncertain.

Children in a class, c. 1939, organized by the Jewish community in Prague after Jews were denied access to public schools. *TM #88415*

In children, the nation is eternal.

Czech aphorism

A group of unknown teens   *TM #88435*

**Teacher Marie Krieshoferová with her students:
Tomás Kohner, Petr Krämer, Stanislav Seiner and
Tomás Huler. Only one from this group survived.**
TM #A8268

▶ Anna Singer
Pastel, pencil
Born December 20, 1931
Deported to Terezín
December 2, 1942
Deported to Auschwitz
December 15, 1944
Perished

The Jewish Museum, Prague, #131.833

176

Around me I see the empty beds
the beds of forty-two living boys
until the order came: the expected transport
now they must go

Called by their names one by one
forty-two delicate pairs of freezing legs
formed up in a line, each with his rucksack
now they are gone

Boys who played and laughed and quarreled
and wept when struck by the thought of
home they wanted to live, were full of
longings imprisoned in the ghetto

Bare shabby sacks of straw
where still this morning the boys lay
forty-two cheerful boys alive
empty beds

Paul Aron Sandfort, a Danish child
deported to Theresienstadt
October 26, 1943

Kamil and Robert Sattler *JMP #32.033*

Norma and Liane Bick *TM #18558*

František Bass *JMP #32.934*

Tomás Reitmann *JMP #33.874*

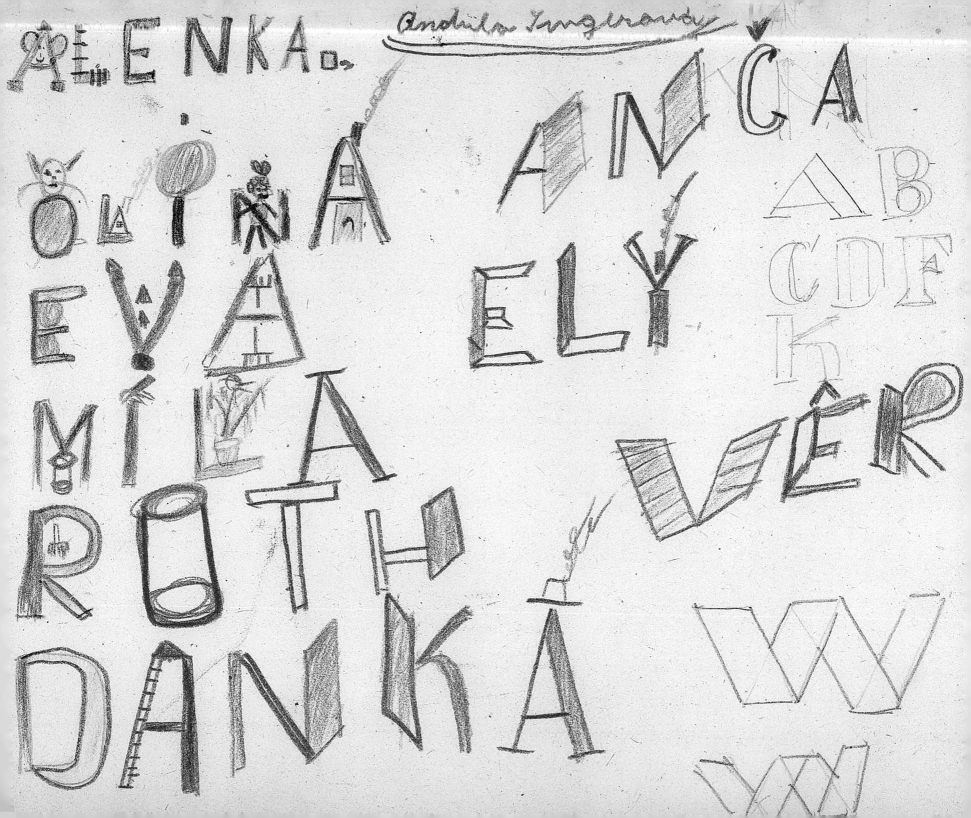

Human memory is a marvelous but deceptive tool. . . . The unreliability of our memories will be fully explained only when we know in what language, in what alphabet, the memories are written: on which material, with what pen they are recorded; and this is a goal that is still very remote.

Primo Levi, "The Memory of Offense," in Geoffrey Hartman, ed., *Bitburg in Moral and Political Perspective* (Bloomington: Indiana University Press, 1986), 130.

Photograph by R. Brosshrová
View of Terezín, 1988
Collection of Ela Weissberger

VOJTĚCH BLODIG

The fortress of Terezín was built during the reign of Joseph II, Hapsburg Emperor (1765–90), and was named after his mother Maria Theresa; the construction of the military installations and fortifications took eleven years. At the time of its construction the Terezín fortress was one of the most advanced defense systems in Europe. It comprised the Main Fortress, the Small Fortress, as well as the fortified space between the New and Old Ohre Rivers. Terezín became an independent royal town and the construction of houses inside the Main Fortress was allowed by imperial permit letters of December 9, 1792.

In 1866, the course of the Austrian-Prussian war showed that the fortress had lost all strategic importance. The imperial statute of the fortress was revoked in October 1888, but the troops stayed in the town and continued to play an important role in its economic, social, and political development. Its inhabitants numbered more than 3,000 at the turn of the century. Originally, Terezín was a predominantly German town; however its share of Czech inhabitants grew rapidly, outnumbering the Germans by the early twentieth century. During World War I, large camps for prisoners-of-war were built there. The Small Fortress, which formerly had been a prison for both political and military prisoners, was then used for confinement purposes even more intensively. Gavrilo Princip, who on June 28, 1914 assassinated Archduke Franz Ferdinand and his wife Countess Sophia in Sarajevo—touching off World War I—was imprisoned there during the war.

With the creation of an independent Czechoslovakia, Terezín started to become an authentic Czech town, and there were significant developments in cultural, political and social life of the town.

The war years 1939–45 were the most tragic in the history of Terezín. In June 1940, a police prison of the Prague Gestapo was established in the Small Fortress, where more than 32,000 prisoners passed through, and more than 2,600 were tortured to death. The town itself was transformed into a ghetto-concentration camp for Jewish prisoners, as the first German relocation transports arrived in November 1941. The Nazis forced the remaining Czech inhabitants to leave the town during the first half of 1942, when Terezín became one large prison. In total, approximately 35,000 people died there; of the 87,000 prisoners who were deported to the extermination camps in the East, roughly 3,800 survived to see liberation. In addition to Jews from Bohemia and Moravia, there were victims of racial persecution from Germany, Austria, the Netherlands, Denmark, Slovakia, and Hungary. At the end of the war, "evacuation transports" from Nazi concentration camps that had been closed brought prisoners from many other countries. Nearly 140,000 Jewish men, women and children had passed through Terezín before it was liberated by the advancing Soviet Army on May 8, 1945.

Repairs of damage caused during its occupation were not possible until the end of the typhoid and spotted fever epidemic which broke out at the end of the war and lasted for weeks after the liberation. Former Terezín inhabitants as well as new settlers started to arrive only in 1946 when a military garrison was again established there.

In September 1945, the National Cemetery was founded in front of the Small Fortress. A funeral for the victims found in mass graves in the Small Fortress and a memorial ceremony, which was organized a year later, marked the beginning of a tradition of solemn annual ceremonies held in the memory of victims of racial and political persecution.

The Terezín Memorial itself was founded on May 6, 1947, when the Czechoslovak government passed a resolution establishing the Memorial of National Suffering in the Small Fortress area. The Museum of Oppression was officially opened on June 11, 1949, with permanent displays designed by the Military Historical Institute in Prague. In that same year the National Cemetery, the Jewish cemetery, and crematorium, as well as the Russian cemetery for POWs of World War I were attached to the Memorial. In addition, a section of the Ohre River, where the ashes of some 22,000 victims of the Jewish ghetto had been thrown into the water on Nazi orders in 1944, was designated as part of the Memorial. The layout of the Terezín Memorial was established in the late 1960s when a section of the underground factory and crematorium with adjacent premises of the former concentration camp in nearby Litoměřice (Leitmeritz) were then added.

As early as 1952, the project to establish a permanent exhibit commemorating the suffering of the Jewish inmates of Terezín during Nazi occupation was initiated. An appropriate building in the town was chosen, however the project leaders eventually decided to install the displays as part of the permanent exhibit in the Small Fortress. The subject of the Jewish ghetto proved difficult to fit into the prevailing ideological themes of

Photograph by Jill Schwab
Street in the ghetto
Terezín, 2000

the Czech Communist regime. The anti-Zionist—in practice anti-Semitic—political policies of that period made any presentation of Jewish suffering very difficult. But the distortions did not end there; for example, any reference to non-Communist resistance during the war was suppressed. As in other areas of Czech life, the history of Terezín had to be subordinated to the needs of the Communist regime.

Change came, however, in the second half of the 1960s, when the foundation for future documentary activity as historical research were established. A library, archives, and photo library were established and systematic training of docents began—in addition to consistent presentation of collections and cooperation with artists dealing with World War II and its victims. In 1968, a plan was elaborated to establish a Memorial in the building of the former Terezín Town school which was used as a "home for boys" aged ten to fifteen during the existence of the ghetto. Once again, the request to create a permanent exhibit commemorating the victims of the Terezín ghetto was crushed by the "normalization" process following the 1968 Soviet invasion of Czechoslovakia. During "normalization," authorities installed instead the "Museum of the National Security Forces and Revolutionary Tradition of North Bohemia" which was, in fact, intended to prevent the creation of the Ghetto Museum

Even among the victims one can observe a manifold alteration of memories; but in this case there is no deliberate intention to deceive. He who is struck by offense or injustice has no need to elaborate a lie to relieve himself of a fault he has not committed, but his innocence does not preclude a distortion of his remembrances.

Primo Levi, "The Memory of Offense," in Geoffrey Hartman, ed., *Bitburg in Moral and Political Perspective* (Bloomington: Indiana University Press, 1986), 134.

Photograph by James Hauser
Interior of crematorium
Terezín, 1999
The Jewish cemetery and crematorium contains mass graves and individual graves. More than 9,000 prisoners were buried there during the first year of the ghetto's existence. The crematorium was also use for those who had died in the Small Fortress and the Litoměřice concentration camp. It is believed that about 50,000 people were cremated there 1942 and 1945. The monument with a symbolic menorah was erected after the war.

182

Photograph by James Hauser
Hallway of the girl's dormitory
L410, Terezín, 1999

in Terezín, which authorities did not want to overtly ban. Many new projects were altered, as the activities of the Memorial had to comply with Communist ideology.

However, for Czech authorities a complete throwback to the past was no longer tenable. Although it was then impossible to establish the Ghetto Museum in Terezín, the staff of the Memorial collected documentary materials about the history of the ghetto and undertook relevant historical research, without which the Memorial could not have been created later that year.

November 1989, when the Communist regime collapsed and Václav Havel was elected president, was a turning point in the history of Czechoslovakia that laid the groundwork for the implementation of the original project for the Memorial. The first task was formally to establish the Ghetto Museum in Terezín; 1991 marked the fiftieth anniversary of the creation of the Terezín Ghetto, and was selected as a target opening date. Through the efforts of new leadership of the Terezín Memorial supported by the organization of former ghetto inmates, the new museum was opened in October 1991.

After the completion of the Terezín Memorial project, new historical research and the phased installation of new exhibits began, a new exhibit about the history of the Gestapo police prison was established within Small

Fortress. A new exhibit at the crematorium of the Jewish cemetery was also needed, as well as the exhibitions "Terezín 1780–1939" and "Litoměřice Concentration Camp 1944–1945." In addition, the permanent "Art Exhibition of the Terezín Memorial" was established with art works reflecting World War II and Nazi racial and political persecution. It was also inevitable that a permanent exhibit "Detention Camp for Germans, Small Fortress 1945–1948" was established as well.

In 1993, the Department of Education of the Terezín Memorial was established which now administers programs for teachers and students from the Czech Republic and abroad. In 1997, part of the reconstructed former Magdeburg barracks, which was formerly the seat of the "Self-Government" of the Ghetto was opened to the public. The Memorial's meeting center was located there, as well as the so-called theater in the attic/lecture hall which is used also for concerts, theater performances, and other cultural events. The barracks also houses the department of collections and permanent exhibitions dedicated to diverse parts of the cultural life of the Terezín Ghetto that includes an exhibit showing the living conditions of the inmates in a reconstructed mass dormitory.

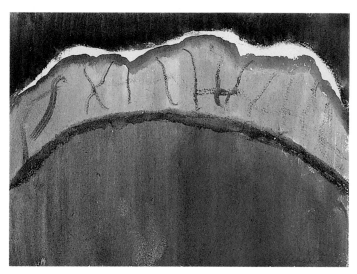

Josef Novak
Watercolor on paper
Born October 25, 1931
Deported to Terezín
April 24, 1942
Deportation to Auschwitz
May 18, 1944
Perished
The Jewish Museum, Prague
#131.675

The Terezín Memorial represents today the only institution of its kind in the Czech Republic. Originally an organization looking after the sites linked to the memory of victims of political and racial persecution in the years of Nazi occupation of Czech lands, the Memorial's activities have evolved and gradually given rise to a major center of research, education, and museum-related programs—an institution which is an acknowledged partner of martyrological centers worldwide. In the past few years especially, its role as a meeting place for people of different nationalities, religions, and political views has been systematically emphasized. The creation of the Terezín Memorial's meeting center has created new opportunities for young people in particular.

184

The landmarks and memorial sites administered by the Terezín Memorial are also a tribute to engineering in Europe at the end of the eighteen century. Visitors to the Small Fortress in Terezín, which housed the police prison of the Prague Gestapo between 1940 and 1945, can view the comprehensively fortified complex. Also, the Terezín Ghetto itself, established in 1941, was surrounded by similar fortification walls. Remains of another concentration camp from the years 1944–45 in the town of Litoměřice are open to visitors; however only the crematorium and its surroundings have survived from this camp, while the premises of the underground factories with code names Richard I and Richard II—where inmates from the camp had to work—are now closed to the public.

Many short-term documentary and art exhibitions are also mounted. Researchers who have access to the collections department and documentation can also use the services of the specialized library. The staff of the Terezín Memorial also provide consultations on matters of racial and political persecution in the Czech lands during World War II, supplying information on the fate of the former inmates of Terezín and Litoměřice. In addition, the Terezín Memorial is implementing significant project in documentation, preservation of collections, and historical research.

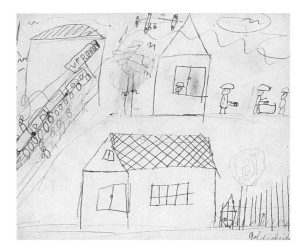

Hana Goldscheider
Pencil on paper
Born December 29, 1931
Deported to Terezín
December 22, 1942
Survived
The Jewish Museum, Prague
#131.628

Terezin Memorial offers tours of landmarks and memorial sites of the former ghetto, the Small Fortress, and of the crematorium in the former concentration camp in Litoměřice. The following permanent exhibits may also be visited:

Ghetto Museum
Terezín in "The Final Solution of the Jewish Question" 1941–1945; A Reconstruction of the Prisoners' Dormitory at the Time of the Ghetto

Magdeburg Barracks
Music in the Terezín Ghetto; Art in the Terezín Ghetto; Literary work in the Terezín Ghetto

Small Fortress Museum
The Terezín Small Fortress 1940–1945; The Art Exhibition of the Terezín Memorial; The Litoměřice Concentration Camp; Terezín 1780–1939; The Detention Camp for Germans, The Small Fortress 1945–1948

Crematorium of the Jewish Cemetery
Mortality and Burial in the Terezín Ghetto

Photograph by R. Brosshrová
Train tracks at Terezín, 1988
Collection of Ela Weissberger

The best way to resist the invasion of painful memories is to prevent their entry into consciousness, to draw a cordon sanitaire all around. It is easier to impede the input of a remembrance than to get rid of it after it is recorded.

Primo Levi, "The Memory of Offense," in Geoffrey Hartman, ed., *Bitburg in Moral and Political Perspective* (Bloomington: Indiana University Press, 1986), 134.

Photograph by James Hauser
The Jewish cemetery
Terezín, 1999

Art, Music and Education as Strategies for Survival: Theresienstadt 1941–45

186

THE JEWISH MUSEUM IN PRAGUE
CZECH REPUBLIC

Works by Friedl Dicker-Brandeis (1898–1944)

Mother Nursing Her Child, Charcoal on paper

Landscape with a Lake, Charcoal on paper

Mountain Landscape, Charcoal on paper

Portrait of a Woman, Charcoal and pencil on paper

Self-Portrait, Charcoal on paper

Portrait of a Man with a Moustache,
(Walter Gropius ?), Charcoal on paper

Portrait of Vera Sormová, Oil on canvas

Double Portrait in a Park, Oil on canvas

Portrait of a Woman I, Pastel on paper

Portrait of a Woman II, Watercolor on paper

Portrait of a Woman Reading, Pastel on paper

Portrait of a Woman with Yellow Sweater Smoking
a Cigarette, Pastel on paper

Flowers (Petunias, etc.), Watercolor and colored ink on paper

Bunch of Tulips in a Glass Vase, Pastel on paper

Landscape, Oil on canvas

Untitled Drawings by Children in Terezín

Josef Bauml, Pencil

Josef Bauml, Watercolor

Anna Brichtá, Collage

Anna Brichtá, Watercolor

Anna Brichtá, Collage with pencil and watercolor

Walter Eisner, Collage

Anna Flach (Hanusová), Pencil

Alice Guttmann, Pencil

Ruth Gutmann, Collage

Ivo Hanuš Kauders, Pencil

Ivo Katz, Watercolor and pencil

Marta Kende, Collage

Hanuš Klauber, Watercolor

Eva Kohn , Collage with watercolor

Lenka Lindt, Collage

Hana Neufeld, Watercolor

Robert Perl, Pastel

Marianna Rosenzweig, Collage

Ruth Schächter, Collage

Egon Seidel, Watercolor

Alice Sittig, Collage

Alice Sittig and Gertruda Kerstenová, Collage with pencil

Erika Stranská, Collage

Hanna Wertheimer (Weingarten), Collage

Eva Wollsteiner, Collage with pencil

Kurt Wurzel, Pencil

Unknown Child Artist, Watercolor

Unknown Child Artist, Watercolor

Unknown Child Artist, Pencil

Unknown Child Artist, Collage with pencil

and seventy-two facsimilies of drawings by children in Terezín

NATIONAL MUSEUM
THEATRE HISTORY DEPARTMENT
PRAGUE, CZECH REPUBLIC

Stage and Costume Designs by František Zelenka

Costume of Vasta for "Esther," India ink and gouache

Costume of Kat for "Esther," India ink and gouache

Costume of King for "Esther," India ink and gouache

Costume of Paris for Cabaret "Karussell" India ink and gouache

Costume of Woman for Cabaret "Karussell,"
India ink and watercolor

Costumes of Woman and Man for Cabaret "Karussell,"
India ink and gouache

Stage design for Cabaret "Karussell" (Window),
India ink and gouache

Stage design for Cabaret "Karussell" (Portal),
India ink and gouache

Stage design for "The Straw Hat," India ink and watercolor

Stage design for "The Last Cyclist,"
India ink and watercolor

Stage design for "The Emperor of Atlantis,"
India ink and watercolor

SIMON WIESENTHAL MUSEUM OF TOLERANCE
LOS ANGELES, CALIFORNIA
Works by Friedl Dicker-Brandeis

Head of a Woman, Pastel

Through Window/Studio, Pastel

People in Bunk Beds, Pencil

Head of a Woman, Charcoal

Two Figures, Pastel

Nude, Pencil

Work by Otto Ungar

Terezín Yard

Work by J.M.

Terezín Fortress, Painting on sugar box lid

Work by Soná Shuk

Heads of Girls, Charcoal

Ephemera

Postcard to Friedl Dicker-Brandeis

Package Notification Card

Clothing Coupons

Letter to Elly

Ghetto Health Card

Czech Registration Card

Savings Bankbook

Receipt of Package Card

Letter to Mrs. Weil

A. E. F. Deported Person Registration Card

I D Document–Amsterdam

THE LEO BAECK INSTITUTE
NEW YORK, NEW YORK
Works by Norbert Troller (1900–81)

Accordion, Lead pencil on blue speckled paper

Latrine, Theresienstadt, Watercolor, pen and ink

Terezín, Men's Quarters, Watercolor and pencil

Brno: Transport to Terezín, Watercolor

Children's Transport, Terezín, Charcoal on paper

Barracks "Dresden" Compound, Pencil on paper

Transport, Terezín, Lead pencil on wove paper

Terezín, Transport Group of People, Pencil

Terezín, Baron, Charcoal

Terezín Figures, Pen and ink (three drawings, 10a–c)

Terezín Dream: My Nightmare, Watercolor on paper

Theatre Performance "Jederman," Barracks "Magdeburg,"
Lead pencil on wove paper

Hannover Barracks, Concert in Compound, Soft lead pencil

Terezín: That's Girka, Charcoal on paper with ink text

Terezín: Man, Marodha, Watercolor on paper

Works by Josef Spier (1900–78)

Terezín: The Deportation Train, Watercolor, pen and ink and
watercolor wash

Young Girl–Terezín, Lead pencil on wove paper

Terezín Transport, Watercolor, pen and ink on paper

GEORG SCHROM COLLECTION
VIENNA, AUSTRIA
Works by Friedl Dicker-Brandeis

Atelier Singer-Dicker, *Garden Room—Hatschek,
perspective drawing*, 1927, Pencil, colored pencil,
and tempera on cardboard

Atelier Singer-Dicker, *Garden Room—Hatschek*, 1927,
Pencil and watercolor on paper

Atelier Singer-Dicker, *Stack of Drawers for Sheet Music, Apartment
Alice Moller*, 1928, Ink, pencil, and colored pencil on paper

Three Ducks, 1921, Lithograph
Plant, c. 1920–29, Pencil on paper
Atelier Singer-Dicker, *Color Specifications for Anteroom, Apartment Dr. Heller,* 1929, Pencil and tempera on tracing paper
Friedl Dicker and Franz Singer, *Costume Designs for Shakespeare's "The Merchant of Venice,"* 1923, (ten black-and-white prints, 7a–j)
Atelier Singer-Dicker, *Table and Chair for Margit Adler,* axonometric view, 1927, Pencil, colored pencil, and tempera on tracing paper
Atelier Singer-Dicker, *Chair and Dressing Table,* 1927, Pencil, colored pencil, and tempera on paper

**BEIT THERESIENSTADT
GIVAT HAIM-IHUD, ISRAEL**
Erna Bonn, *Two Dolls*
Oswald Pöck, *Monopoly Game*
Unknown Child Artist, *Toy Animal,* Cotton batting

**JOŽA KARAS COLLECTION,
HARTFORD, CONNECTICUT**
Works by Otto Ungar
Portrait of Hans Krása, Charcoal
Hospital Ward in Theresienstadt, Watercolor

**ELA STEIN WEISSBERGER COLLECTION
TAPPAN, NEW YORK**
Max Plaček, *Portrait of Otto Altenstein,* Colored pencil
Walter Weiss, designs for jewelry, Pencil on tracing paper
Walter Weiss, *Views of Terezín from Clock Tower,* Five photographs
Rudy Brösshrová, *Terezín: Railroad to the East,* Photograph, 1981
Rudy Brösshrová, *View of Terezín, L410,* Photograph, 1981
Ela Stein, *Terezín coat-of-arms,* Wood

Theresienstadt currency
Star of David, Cloth
Ghetto Health Card
Ghetto Work Card
Package Receipt Card

**ANNA FLACH HANUSOVÁ COLLECTION
BRNO, CZECH REPUBLIC**
Fragment of cloth flag and felt fascimile
Brooch, "The Trio," Copper
Release form to perform in *Brundibár,* fascimile

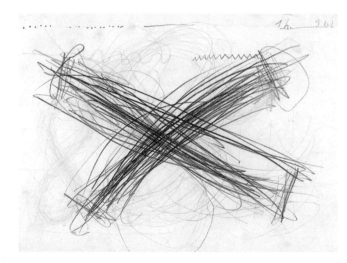

Ruth Hein
Pencil
Born February 19, 1934
Deported to Terezín
July 30, 1942
Deported to Auschwitz
October 23, 1944
Perished
The Jewish Museum, Prague
#131.665v

Renata Kitty Fiallová
Pencil and crayon on paper
Born November 14, 1932
Deported to Terezín
September 8, 1942
Survived

The Jewish Museum, Prague
#133.235

CONTRIBUTORS

Ruth Weiss
Pencil on paper
Born March 16, 1931
Deported to Terezín
November 20, 1942
Deported to Auschwitz
May 18, 1944
Perished
The Jewish Museum, Prague
#121.599v

VOJTĚCH BLODIG is the Deputy Director, Terezín Ghetto Memorial Museum, Terezín, Czech Republic. He studied history at the Faculty of Philosophy of Charles University in Prague between 1964 and 1969. He concentrated on the subject of fascism and anti-fascism in the period 1933 to 1938. Later, he focused on questions of political persecution and the genocide of the Jews in the period from 1939 to 1945. He has published several articles on these themes.

ANNE D. DUTLINGER, Curator of *Art, Music and Education as Strategies for Survival: Theresienstadt 1941–45*, is Assistant Professor of Art and director of graphic and interactive design studies at Moravian College, Bethlehem, PA. She received an MFA from Yale University School of Art.

MICHAELA HÁJKOVÁ is the Curator of Painting and Graphics Collection, Jewish Museum, Prague, Czech Republic, and serves on the museum's acquisitions committee. She is a member of the Czech Art Recovery Commission, which identifies artwork looted from Czech Jews during World War II.

SUSAN LESHNOFF is Assistant Professor of Fine Arts and coordinator of the Art Education Program at Seton Hall University, New Jersey. She also serves on the Graduate Faculty of the Museum Studies Program. She received her Ed.D. in art education from

Columbia University. She is the author of several articles, including "What is Going on in Elementary Art Classrooms" and "Art, Ambiguity, and Critical Thinking," both published in *Art Education*, the journal of the National Art Education Association.

SYBIL H. MILTON (October 6, 1941–October 16, 2000) was an independent historian and exhibition consultant in Chevy Chase, Maryland. Director of Archives at the Leo Baeck Institute, New York, from 1974 to 1984, she also served as Senior Historian of the United States Holocaust Memorial Museum in Washington from 1986 to 1997. She served as Vice-President of Independent Experts Commission: Switzerland—Second World War. Co-author of *Art of the Holocaust* (1981), which received the National Jewish Book Award in Visual Arts; she also edited and co-authored *Innocence and Persecution: The Art of Jewish Children in Nazi Germany, 1936–1941* (1989). She published a number of important articles on various aspects of the Holocaust, including several articles about the fate of art and artists in Nazi Germany and occupied Europe. Her most recent book is *In Fitting Memory: The Art and Politics of Holocaust Memorials* (1991). In December 1999, she was co-editor and featured author for the special issue "Photography and the Holocaust" of the journal *History of Photography*.

REBECCA ROVIT is a theater historian and co-editor of *Theatrical Performance during the Holocaust: Texts, Documents, Memoirs* (1999). She is the author of several essays that have appeared in such journals as *American Theatre*, *Theatre Survey*, *TDR*, and *Contemporary Theatre Review*. Her current research projects include Northwestern University's upcoming Block Museum exhibition, *The Last Expression: Art from the Archives of Auschwitz.*

HANNELORE WONSCHICK is a freelance journalist and a radio producer/writer in Berlin. Her one hour radio documentary on the history of the children's opera *Brundibár* was released on CD by Edition Abseits in 1999. Interviews and documents in the essay "Coming of Age in Theresienstadt: Friedl's Girls from Room 28" are taken from her forthcoming book *Zimmer 28: Mädchenheim Theresienstadt,* which will be published in 2001 by Campus Verlag, Frankfurt.

Unknown Photographer, June 23, 1944
Comité International de la Croix Rouge.
Copy courtesy U.S. Holocaust Memorial Museum #61.607

On June 23, 1944, The International Red Cross Commission, composed of one Swiss and two Danish representatives, conducted a six-hour tour of the Theresienstadt ghetto. The tour was carefully managed and controlled by the Nazis. During the visit, this group of children was photographed. Shortly afterward, all of the children except Paul Aron Sandfort (third from left) were taken to Auschwitz where they perished. Sandfort was spared by virtue of his Danish citizenship.

SYMPOSIUM AT MORAVIAN COLLEGE

ART, MUSIC AND EDUCATION AS STRATEGIES FOR SURVIVAL: THERESIENSTADT 1941–45
FEBRUARY 10, 2000

OPENING REMARKS
ERVIN ROKKE
President of Moravian College

INTRODUCTION
ANNE D. DUTLINGER
Assistant Professor of Art
Curator, *Art, Music and Education
as Strategies for Survival*

MODERATOR
FRANK BOLDT
Director, Evropské Comenium
Cheb, Czech Republic

KEYNOTE SPEAKER
SYBIL H. MILTON
Author, historian, exhibition consultant
Chevy Chase, MD
Art and Artists in Theresienstadt

VOJTĚCH BLODIG
Deputy Director, Pamatník Terezín
Terezín, Czech Republic
*The Role of Theresienstadt in the
Final Solution*

MICHAELA HÁJKOVÁ
Curator of Painting
and Graphic Collection
Jewish Museum in Prague
*Friedl Dicker-Brandeis—
Lady in a Car*

SUSAN LESHNOFF
Art Educator & Professor
Seton Hall University
Orange, New Jersey
*Holocaust Survival and the Spirit
of the Bauhaus*

CATHY MALCHIODI
Licensed Professional Art Therapist
Educator, editor, *Art Therapy Journal*
Salt Lake City, Utah
The Reparative Power of Children's Art

GEORG SCHROM
Architect, author, designer
Vienna, Austria
2 X Bauhaus in Vienna

REBECCA ROVIT
Theatre historian and author
Bloomington, Indiana
*A Carousel of Theatrical Performances
in Theresienstadt*

ZDENKA ERLICH-FANTLOVÁ
Actress
Survivor of Theresienstadt, Auschwitz,
Mauthausen, and Bergen-Belsen
London, England
Memoir: On Stage in Theresienstadt

THOMAS RIETSCHEL
Artistic Director, Jeunesse Musicales
Weikersheim, Germany
Lessons for Germany from Terezín's Musicians

MARK LUDWIG
Director, Terezín Chamber
Music Foundation
Boston, Massachusetts
*Performance as Remembrance:
Music and Musicians in Terezín*

CLOSING REMARKS
H.E. ALEXANDR VONDRA
Ambassador of the Czech Republic

CONCERT

Silenced Voices:
Music from Theresienstadt

Mark Ludwig, Director & Narrator
The Hawthorne String Quartet
Joy Ondra Hirokawa, Director
Bel Canto Children's Chorus
Ela Stein Weissberger, Terezín

Opening remarks by Larry Lipkis
Professor of Music and Composition
at Moravian College

COMING OF AGE IN THERESIENSTADT:
A PANEL DISCUSSION

FEBRUARY 11, 2000

OPENING REMARKS

H.E. MARTIN BÚTORA
Ambassador of Slovakia
Slovakia's Holocaust Survivors:
Voices and Faces from Testimonies

SUSAN E. CERNYAK-SPATZ
Professor of Foreign Languages,
University of North Carolina
Charlotte, North Carolina
Forgetting for the Future

HANS-MARTIN WUERTH
Professor of German Literature
Moravian College
Advocate for Holocaust education
Children as Victims of the Holocaust

PANEL

LARRY SILBERSTEIN, *Moderator*
Director, Berman Center
for Jewish Studies Lehigh University

PANEL PARTICIPANTS

ELA STEIN WEISSBERGER
Survivor of Theresienstadt L410, Room 28
Student of Friedl Dicker-Brandeis
Cast member of *Brundibár*
Interior designer and educator
Tappan, NY

HELGA WEISSOVÁ-HOSKOVÁ
Survivor of Theresienstadt,
Auschwitz, and Mauthausen
Artist
Prague, Czech Republic

PAUL ARON SANDFORT
Survivor of Theresienstadt
Author and educator
Copenhagen, Denmark

BERND WIEGAND
Director, Niedersächsischer
Verein zur Förderung von
Theresienstadt/Terezín e.V
Advocate for Holocaust education
Rosdorf, Germany

Translations provided
by Sybil H. Milton

FRANK BOLDT is the founder of the Evropské Comenium in Cheb in collaboration with Czech scholars from Prague. He received his doctorate from Prague University where he has lectured since 1993. He has also served as an interpreter for German chancellors and foreign ministers in German-Czechoslovak state conferences. Boldt is the author of more than forty publications on German-Slavonic-Jewish relations and has worked in close cooperation with Czech and Russian dissident writers and scholars.

MARTIN BÚTORA has served as the Slovak ambassador to the United States since his appointment in 1999. Bútora was one of the co-founders of Public Against Violence, the leading Slovak movement in the Velvet Revolution against communism. In 1995–97, he coordinated a research project based on videotestimonies of Holocaust survivors from Slovakia. Dr. Bútora is the author of several books on post-Communist trans-formation, civil society, political behavior, ethnic and nationalism issues, foreign policy issues, and anti-Semitism. He is married to Zora Bútorova, a sociologist and author.

SUSAN E. CERNYAK-SPATZ is Professor Emeritus of the Department of Languages and Culture at the University of North Carolina, Charlotte. A survivor of Theresienstadt and Auschwitz-Birkenau (1943–45), she lectures extensively in the US and Europe. She is the author of numerous articles and books including German Holocaust Literature and a translation of the handwritten memoirs of Norbert Troller, *Theresienstadt: Hitler's Gift to the Jews.*

ZDENKA FANTLOVÁ attended The English Institute in Prague before she was deported to Theresienstadt with her family in 1942. In Theresienstadt she acted in numerous cabarets and plays, and was transported to Auschwitz-Birkenau. From Auschwitz she was sent to do hard labor in Kurzbach, a forced march across the River Oder to Gross Rosen and later went to Mauthausen Concentration Camp. In February, 1945, she was transported to Bergen-Belsen where she was later liberated by British forces. Her entire family perished in the war. Fantlová-Ehrlich has a daughter and is the proud grandmother of two. She lives in London with her family. She lectures frequently throughout Europe.

LARRY LIPKIS is the Bertha Mae Starner '27 and Jay F. Starner Professor of Music and Composer in Residence at Moravian College in Bethlehem, Pennsylvania. He directs the early music activities at the college, which include the Collegium Musicum and the Mostly Monteverdi Ensemble, and also teaches composition and music theory courses. Since 1986, Larry has performed and recorded with the Baltimore Consort, an early music ensemble specializing in popular music of the Renaissance and Baroque eras.

MARK LUDWIG is the director of the Terezín Chamber Music Foundation who has studied the life and work of the Theresienstadt composers. As director of the Foundation, Ludwig has lectured, produced children's programs, and performed with the Hawthorne String Quartet throughout the world.

CATHY MALCHIODI is a licensed art therapist, registered expressive arts therapist, and licensed clinical counselor. She has been appointed as a National Advisory Board member to the Institute for Trauma & Loss in Children (TLC). She is Director of the Institute for the Arts & Health, a national training program in the arts, based in Salt Lake City, Utah, and is the editor of *Art Therapy: Journal of the American Art Therapy Association.* Ms. Malchiodi has published over fifty articles and chapters on the topic of art therapy.

PETER RAFAELI is Honorary Consul-General of the Czech Republic for Pennsylvania and Delaware. Before his appointment as Honorary Consul-General, Rafaeli was an automobile dealer. He currently serves on the board of the American Red Cross, the Old York Road Symphony Society, and SVU (Czechoslovak Society for Arts and Sciences).

THOMAS RIETSCHEL has been the general secretary of Jeunesses Musicales Germany since 1992 and is a member of the board of Jeunesses Musicales International. He has studied literature, cultural science, and violin in Tübingen, Vienna, and Nürnberg and worked several years as a musician and manager of a chamber orchestra. He is also the initiator of the International Brundibár-Project.

PAUL ARON SANDFORT is a Theresienstadt survivor. He is currently a teacher in Denmark. Arrested after trying to flee Denmark to neutral Sweden, he was deported to Theresienstadt where he was interned until April 15, 1945, when he was liberated by the Swedish Red Cross. Sandfort has an M.A. in musicology and German literature and is the author of *Ben the Alien Bird* (Gefen, 1999), a biographical novel.

GEORG SCHROM currently works as a freelance architect in Vienna where he has been with Brandt & Schrom Architekten since 1997. He received his Master of Architecture and Urban Design in 1993 from the Hochschule für Angewandte Kunst in Vienna. His designs include many public and private buildings, urban design projects and exhibitions.

DR. LAURENCE SILBERSTEIN is the Philip and Muriel Berman Professor of Jewish Studies in the Department of Religion Studies, Lehigh University, and director of the Philip and Muriel Berman Center for Jewish Studies. His books include *Martin Buber's Social and Religious Thought: Alienation and the Quest for Meaning* (1989) and *The Postzionist Debates: Knowledge and Power in Israeli Culture* (1999).

ELA WEISSBERGER is a Theresienstadt survivor. She directs and manages an interior design business. She lectures widely on the role of art and music in Theresienstadt, particularly to school groups. Deported to Theresienstadt in 1942, Ela performed the role of "Cat" in over fifty *Brundibár* performances, including the performance filmed for the Nazi propaganda film, *The Führer Gives a Town to the Jews*. After the war she attended art school for ceramics in Prague.

HELGA WEISSOVÁ-HOSKOVÁ is a professional artist who survived Theresienstadt, Auschwitz, and Mauthausen. She is the author of *Zeichne, was Du siehst* (*Draw What You See*, Wallstein Verlag, 1998), a cycle of drawings depicting different aspects of life in the Theresienstadt ghetto which she created while interned there. After the war, she studied at the Academy of Fine Arts in Prague. Hosková's drawings are known throughout the world.

ALEXANDR VONDRA was named Ambassador of the Czech Republic to the United States in 1997. Born in Prague in 1961, he served as foreign policy advisor to President Vaclav Havel from 1990–92. In 1992, he was appointed the First Deputy Minister of International Affairs of the Czech Republic. In January 1993, he was named First Deputy Minister of Foreign Affairs of the Czech Republic. In 1996, he became the chief negotiator for the Czech Republic in the process of preparing the Czech-German Declaration.

BERND WIEGAND is director of Niedersächsischer Verein zur Förderung von Theresienstadt/Terezín e.V (Lower Saxon Association for the Promotion and Preservation of Theresienstadt/Terezín) founded in 1995, which develops cultural events and educational materials about the Holocaust. He is the co-author of *Begleitheft zu der Ausstellung mit Beispielen fur die Einbindung in den Unterricht* (1998) and *Wiegand u.a.: Projektdokumentation Terezín* (1999).

HANS-MARTIN WUERTH teaches German language and literature at Moravian College. His specialty is German literature of the twentieth century. He received his M.A. and Ph.D. degrees from Rutgers University, where he has also taught. Dr. Wuerth has taught courses on National Socialism and the Holocaust, and led over twenty student trips to Europe on the history of the Third Reich

Walter Eisner
Collage (detail)
Born November 3, 1933
Deported to Terezín
November 20, 1942
Deported to Auschwitz
January 20, 1943
Perished
The Jewish Museum, Prague
#133.039

One could not ask for a more ideal setting for the exhibit, concert, and symposium, *Art, Music and Education as Strategies for Survival: Theresienstadt 1941–45* than Moravian College. The Moravian Brethren left Europe as a response to religious intolerance they faced there. In 1740, in Bethlehem, Pennsylvania, they founded a community and Moravian College, an educational institution based on equality and tolerance.

Moravian College continues the mission of its founders in encouraging the love of learning and the creation of a meaningful and purposeful life. The ideas of the great educational reformer and philosopher, Jan Amos Comenius continue to resonate in the vigorous blend of tradition and innovation that are the heart of the liberal arts education at Moravian College.

Comenius, or Komensky, as he is known in his native Czech lands, believed that a just society could be attained through education. Komensky's goal was to create schools in which all students were educated, irrespective of their economic, social, or national status. Komensky taught that true learning required creative engagement rather than forced discipline, and that education would create a more humane society through individual good will and mutual responsibility.[1]

Komensky's vision of a just society and global understanding inspired the establishment of Moravian College, as well as the founding of the United Nations and the United Nations Educational, Scientific and Cultural Organization, UNESCO.[2]

As we begin a new millennium, an international effort is underway to appraise the world we have inherited, understand the world we live in today, and to assess how to establish a more humane and civil society for the future. Providing equal opportunities for education is a key component of how to establish a humanistic foundation for the process of globalization.[3]

Václav Havel, President of the Czech Republic said, "It cannot suffice to invent new machines, new regulations, new institutions. It is necessary to change and improve our understanding of the true purpose of what we are and what we do in the world... to develop new models of behavior, new scales of values and goals, and thereby invest the global regulations treaties and institutions with a new spirit and meaning."[4]

PETER RAFAELI

The exhibition, *Art, Music and Education as Strategies for Survival: Theresienstadt 1941–45*, which opened in February 2000 at the Payne Gallery of Moravian College, exhibited original art and objects from the Czech Republic, Austria, and Israel, many of which had never traveled to the United States. Art created by both children and adults in Terezín, archival photography, and memorabilia from survivors, merged to form a unique and powerful narrative of loss and survival during the Holocaust. Komensky's own theory of how images inspire interest and sustain memory was manifested in the impact made by the art on its many viewers.

The participants at the two-day symposium which accompanied the opening of the exhibition included survivors of Terezín from the Czech Republic, England, Denmark, and the United States; Holocaust scholars and art historians from the Czech Republic and the United States; and individuals from Germany and Austria who work to preserve the memory of those who perished during the Holocaust. A sizable diplomatic delegation attended the symposium, concert, and the opening of the exhibition. The Czech Republic was represented by its Ambassador to the United States, H.E. Alexandr Vondra, the Counselor for Cultural Affairs, Ivan Dubovicky, the Consul-General of the Czech Republic in New York, Petr Gandalovič, and the Director of the Czech Center in New York, Přemsyl Pela. The Slovak Republic was represented by its Ambassador, H.E. Martin Bútora.

To step decisively into the new century, we must recognize how inextricably connected are the nations of the world. The goal of a global civic society strongly echoes the ideas of Komensky— to educate our children, we must teach them to value the lessons of the past and to think critically to apply those lessons to future solutions. To avert the tragic loss of life and destruction of culture seen so vividly in the art from the Jewish ghetto of Terezín, we must inspire the next generation to find peaceful solutions to overcome tyranny and hate.

NOTES

1. Jaroslav Pánek, *Comenius, Teacher of Nations* (Prague: 1991), 30–34

2. Ibid, 76

3. Václav Havel, *Five Step in Hope: Forum 2000* (Prague, 2000), 1

4. Ibid, 1–2

...if we do not stand up to evil at its inception, at its first inconspicuous manifestations, then we risk later we shall no longer be able to stand up to it or we shall be able to resist only through new human sacrifices.... even mere indifference must be resisted.

Václav Havel
Preface, *The Genocide of the Czech Jews*
by Miroslav Karny
(Prague:1992)

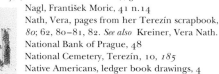

Walter Eisner
Collage
Born November 3, 1933
Deported to Terezín
November 20, 1942
Deported to Auschwitz
January 20, 1943
Perished

The Jewish Museum, Prague #133.039

Details from study of letterforms, pp. 198–203
Anna Singer
Pastel, pencil
Born December 20, 1931
Deported to Terezín December 2, 1942
Deported to Auschwitz December 15, 1944
Perished

The Jewish Museum, Prague #131833

A NOTE ON THE TYPE

The text was set in 10 point ITC New Baskerville with oldstyle figures on 13 point leading. British printer John Baskerville of Birmingham created the types that bear his name around 1752. George Jones designed this version of Baskerville for Linotype-Hell in 1930 and the International Typeface Corporation licensed it in 1982. An excellent text typeface, New Baskerville has a delicacy and grace that come with its long, elegant serifs and the subtle transfer of stroke weight from thick to very thin. ITC New Baskerville is a trademark of International Typeface Corporation.

The text display font is Gill Sans. Designed by Eric Gill and released by the Monotype Corporation between 1928 and 1930, Gill Sans is based on the typeface that Edward Johnston, the innovative British calligrapher and teacher, designed in 1916 for the signs of the London Underground. Gill's alphabet is more classical in proportion and contains his signature flared capital R and eyeglass lowercase g. With distinct roots in pen-written letters, Gill Sans is classified as a humanist sans serif. Gill Sans is a trademark of The Monotype Corporation.

Page numbers and panel text are set in Frutiger. Designed by Adrian Frutiger in 1963, its robust legibility is favored for architectural signage as well as books. Frutiger is a registered trademark of Linotype-Hell AG.

Composed by Anne D. Dutlinger and Stephanie Frey
Moravian College Design Lab
Bethlehem, Pennsylvania

Printed and bound in Hong Kong
by C & C Offset Printing Co., Ltd.

Věra Wurzelová
Colored pencil
Born December 10, 1930
Deported to Terezín
July 13, 1942
Deported to Auschwitz
Survived
The Jewish Museum, Prague
#131.800r